# 101
## —BEST—
## VEGAN
## FOODS

Publications International, Ltd.

Photography on pages 7, 13, 53, 117 and 165 by PIL Photo Studio, Chicago.
**Photographer:** Justin Paris
**Photographer's Assistant:** Annemarie Zelasko
**Food Stylists:** Amy Andrews, Carol Smoler
**Assistant Stylists:** Lissa Levy, Breanna Moeller

All recipes and recipe photographs copyright © Publications International, Ltd.

Recipe development on pages 13, 25, 117, 143, 163 and 165 by Carissa Kinyon.

Recipe development on pages 7, 53, 63 and 65 by Marilyn Pocius.

Contributing writers: Carissa Kinyon and Marilyn Pocius

**Recipes pictured on the front cover:** Lentil Stew over Couscous *(page 59)* and Vegan Pesto *(page 25).*

**Recipe pictured on the back cover:** Caribbean Sweet Potato and Bean Stew *(page 11).*

**Photo Credits**

**Front Cover:** PIL Collection (left and right); Shutterstock (center).

**Back Cover:** PIL Collection (bottom); Shutterstock (top).

**Interior Art:** Dreamstime, Fotofolio, iStockphoto, PIL Collection, Shutterstock and Thinkstockphotos

ISBN-13: 978-1-4508-5125-1
ISBN-10: 1-4508-5125-8

Library of Congress Control Number: 2012934846

Manufactured in China.

8 7 6 5 4 3 2 1

**Nutritional Analysis:** Every effort has been made to check the accuracy of the nutritional information that appears with each recipe. However, because numerous variables account for a wide range of values for certain foods, nutritive analyses in this book should be considered approximate. Different results may be obtained by using different nutrient databases and different brand-name products.

**Microwave Cooking:** Microwave ovens vary in wattage. Use the cooking times as guidelines and check for doneness before adding more time.

**Note:** This book is for informational purposes and is not intended to provide medical advice. Neither Publications International, Ltd., nor the author, editors, or publisher take responsibility for any possible consequences from any treatment, procedure, exercise, dietary modification, action, or application of medication or preparation by any person reading or following the information in this book. The publication of this book does not constitute the practice of medicine, and this book does not attempt to replace your physician, pharmacist, or other health care provider. **Before undertaking any course of treatment, the author, editors, and publisher advise the reader to check with a physician or other health care provider.**

Publications International, Ltd.

# The Delights of Vegan Cooking

Vegan, at least as defined for this book, means consuming no animal products—no meat, poultry, fish, dairy, eggs or honey. There are many different kinds of vegans and even more reasons for becoming one, from ethics to weight control.

Of course there are plenty of compelling health and environmental reasons for giving up animal products, but one of the unsung joys of cooking vegan dishes is the incredible flavors you'll discover. There is so much variety in terms of color, taste and texture in the plant kingdom. When a meal isn't centered around meat, it's easier to appreciate the sweet tenderness of a roasted beet or the crunch of just-picked sugar snap peas. The foods in this book were chosen to help make vegan cooking and eating not just healthy, but truly delicious.

## Vegan Goes Mainstream

Gone are the days when a vegan had to visit a strange smelling, brightly lit health food store to buy provisions. Now any decent size market stocks soymilk, quinoa, veggie burgers and even seitan. A recent study estimates that 3.2 percent of the adults in the U.S. (about 7.3 million people) follow a vegetarian-based diet. Estimates put the number of vegans in that pool at about 1 million (and growing fast!). Millions more simply want the benefits of a vegan diet but aren't ready to commit to it 100 percent.

Whether you've been a hardcore vegan for decades or you're just interested in experimenting with a plant-based diet, this book was written to inspire you to cook with new ingredients and to open up a world of flavor and enjoyment.

page 109

page 75

page 51

# The Healthy Vegan Diet

The key to any healthy diet is variety. A vegan diet consisting of pasta and french fries would certainly not provide the vitamins, minerals and other nutrients human bodies need. A diet of fast food burgers, fried chicken and soda would be even worse! For vegans, variety means including fruits, vegetables, leafy greens, whole grains, nuts, seeds and legumes.

## The Protein Problem That Isn't

If you've been a vegan for a while, you've probably been asked, "But what do you do about protein?" Our meat-centric society thinks of beef, pork, chicken and milk as the only good sources of protein. Plant foods provide plenty of protein. Check the nutritional listings for tofu, lentils or quinoa if you need reassurance.

Decades ago it was believed that since meat contained all the essential amino acids (the ones our body can't produce on its own), vegetarians needed to eat a combination of foods at each meal that provided this same assortment. It was complicated and soon found to be totally unnecessary—your metabolism takes care of combining for you. In fact most Americans eat too much protein, which can be unhealthy!

## What about Vitamin B12 and Calcium?

This essential vitamin is found only in animal foods. Fortunately there are many vegan foods that are fortified with B12. Soymilk, other dairy-free milks, cereals, nutritional yeast and meat substitutes may be fortified, but check labels. It's also possible to take a B12 supplement. Calcium is found in dark green vegetables, tofu, tahini and blackstrap molasses as well in some fortified foods. Check the chart for more information.

---

## Know Your Nutrients

Here's a list of good sources of nutrients sometimes lacking in a vegan diet.

| Protein | Omega-3 Fatty Acids |
|---|---|
| legumes | flaxseed |
| lentils | olive oil |
| soy products | tofu |
| whole grains | walnuts |
| **Calcium** | **Iron\*** |
| almonds | brussels sprouts |
| broccoli | blackstrap molasses |
| fortified orange juice | edamame |
| kale | kidney beans |
| tahini | lentils |
| tofu | turmeric |
| **Vitamin B12** | \*To enhance iron absorption, combine these foods with those rich in Vitamin C. |
| enriched dairy-free milks | |
| enriched nutritional yeast | |
| fortified cereals | |

# Tips to Keep Your Vegan Diet Interesting

page 17

**1.** Serve three or four small plates instead of one main course with sides.

**2.** Go ethnic. Explore Asian noodle dishes like Szechuan Vegetable Lo Mein (page 17) or try Mexican bean dishes like Four-Pepper Black Bean Fajitas (page 29).

**3.** Give potatoes and pasta a rest. Try adding couscous (pages 58–59), quinoa (page 140) or bulgur wheat (pages 42–43) instead.

pages 166–167

**4.** Experiment with meat replacements. In addition to tofu (pages 166–167), try tempeh (pages 162–163),  seitan (pages 142–143) or texturized soy protein (pages 164–165).

**5.** Cook with the seasons. Take advantage of farmers' markets and enjoy more fresh produce.

**6.** Get beyond broccoli. Try a new vegetable. How about tomatillos (pages 168–169) or parsnips (pages 128–129)?

page 66

**7.** Spice things up with chipotle peppers (page 30), curry paste (page 66), ginger (pages 88–89) or jalapeños (pages 90–91).

page 29

pages 120–121

# Agar Agar

This amazing ingredient thickens liquid like gelatin only it's made from seaweed. Agar agar has been used for centuries in Asian cuisines to create beautiful molded desserts, jellies, puddings and other dishes.

## benefits

Anything gelatin can do, agar agar (often called just agar) can do better and without animal products. Unlike gelatin, agar will set at room temperature and stay set even when warm, up to about 85°F. It has little taste of its own so it works well in sweet or savory dishes. In addition, agar does retain some of the beneficial nutrients of seaweed.

## selection and storage

You'll find agar in many health or natural food stores stocked with vegan or seaweed products like nori. Agar is most commonly available in flake or powder form, but also comes in sticks or bars, which are more time consuming to use since they take longer to dissolve. In Japanese cuisine agar is called kanten and you may also find it labeled Chinese gelatin or Chinese grass.

## preparation

To substitute agar flakes for gelatin you'll need more. One tablespoon of gelatin or two tablespoons of agar will set about two cups of liquid. The powdered form is more concentrated so you will only need one teaspoon per cup of liquid. Acidic ingredients or those containing oxalic acid, such as chocolate, spinach and rhubarb, interfere with gelling and require more agar. A smaller amount can be used to thicken sauces, mousses and puddings.

## recipe suggestions

Agar gels so quickly that layering different flavors or suspending fruit or vegetables is easier than it would be with gelatin. Use agar to make fruit juice molds. (Stay away from raw pineapple, kiwi or papaya. They contain enzymes that can prevent gelling.) Add tofu or dairy-free yogurt to create a sweet or savory mousse. Pour a thin layer of a fruit juice cooked with agar into a shallow pan. Once it sets, cut it into squares or other shapes to use as a garnish or in a fruit salad.

# vegan veggie terrine

6 cups water

2 leeks, coarsely chopped

2 celery stalks, coarsely chopped

1 carrot, coarsely chopped

5 cloves garlic

2 sprigs *each* fresh parsley, thyme, basil
and cilantro

1 tablespoon kosher salt

1 tablespoon whole peppercorns

3 tablespoons agar agar flakes

Assorted blanched and/or roasted
vegetables, such as yellow beets,
asparagus, carrots and/or broccoli

2 roasted red bell peppers (jarred or fresh)

1 tablespoon assorted minced herbs

Salt and black pepper

1. For broth, combine water, leeks, celery, carrot, garlic, herb sprigs, salt and peppercorns in large saucepan. Bring to a boil, reduce heat to medium and simmer 30 minutes. Strain broth; discard solids. Return to saucepan.

2. Sprinkle agar over broth; stir and bring to a boil. Reduce heat to medium; simmer, stirring frequently, 5 minutes or until agar flakes are dissolved. Transfer to large measuring cup.

3. Meanwhile prepare vegetables. Slice beets, trim asparagus to fit loaf pan, break broccoli into small florets. Pat vegetables dry and season with salt and pepper.

4. Pour a very thin layer of agar into 8×4-inch loaf pan. Refrigerate 5 minutes or until set. Arrange layer of vegetables on top of agar. Sprinkle with herbs. Pour agar to cover; return pan to refrigerator until set. Continue making layers of vegetables, herbs and agar, refrigerating after each layer until set. If agar in measuring cup solidifies, return to saucepan and reheat, stirring to dissolve. Refrigerate terrine until ready to serve.

*Makes 8 appetizer servings*

## nutrients per serving:

**Calories** 42
**Calories from Fat** 5%
**Protein** 1g
**Carbohydrate** 9g
**Fiber** 2g
**Total Fat** <1g
**Saturated Fat** 0g
**Cholesterol** 0mg
**Sodium** 777mg

# Agave Syrup

Agave syrup or nectar is a natural sweetener made from the tropical white or blue agave plant, a cactus-like succulent. For vegans, agave's delicate flavor and syrupy consistency make it an excellent substitute for honey.

## benefits

Since honey comes from bees, most vegans avoid it. Agave (pronounced uh-GAH-vee or uh-GAH-vay) is not only a delicious substitute, it offers some advantages of its own. Because it can be processed at very low temperatures, agave is usually considered a raw food. It also has a lower glycemic index than sugar so it is less likely to cause a spike in your blood sugar. While it does have more nutrients than highly refined white sugar, like any sweetener it should be used in moderation.

## selection and storage

Agave has become trendy and most supermarkets and natural foods stores now offer a choice of brands as well as dark or light versions. Dark agave is generally more flavorful. Raw organic agave is the least processed. All agave can be stored at room temperature in a cool, dark place for up to a year.

## preparation

Agave can be substituted one-to-one for honey, though it is a bit sweeter and has a milder flavor with more caramel or toffee notes than most honey. You can easily substitute smaller amounts of agave for regular granulated sugar in drinks, salad dressings and sauces. Both agave and sugar have about the same number of calories per teaspoon. Since agave is about one and one half times sweeter, you'll use less and consume fewer calories. In baking recipes, substituting agave for sugar is a bit trickier. For every cup of sugar, try using ⅔ cup of agave and reducing other liquids by at least ¼ cup to make up for the moisture difference. Baked goods may brown more quickly, too, so watch carefully and reduce the oven temperature if needed.

## recipe suggestions

For sweetening tea or coffee, lighter grades of agave are a neutral sweetener. Darker agave is an excellent addition to barbecue sauce, stews and the like where a more robust flavor is welcome.

# vegan pancakes

2 cups soymilk or other dairy-free milk
2 tablespoons lemon juice
2 tablespoons vegetable oil
1 tablespoon agave syrup
1 cup all-purpose flour
1 cup spelt flour
1 teaspoon baking soda
1 teaspoon baking powder
½ teaspoon salt
1 to 2 tablespoons dairy-free margarine, melted
Fresh fruit and maple syrup

1. Combine soymilk and lemon juice in large measuring cup. Set aside 5 minutes or until milk curdles. Stir in oil and agave.

2. Whisk together all-purpose flour, spelt flour, baking soda, baking powder and salt in large bowl. Whisk in soymilk mixture until fairly smooth. (Some lumps will remain.)

3. Heat large nonstick skillet or griddle over medium-high heat. Brush lightly with margarine. Pour batter onto skillet in 4 inch circles. Cook 3 to 5 minutes or until edges of pancake become dull and bubbles form on top. Flip pancakes and cook 1 to 2 minutes or until browned. Keep warm.

4. Serve with fresh fruit and maple syrup.

*Makes about 14 pancakes*

## nutrients per pancake:

**Calories** 104
**Calories from Fat** 32%
**Protein** 3g

**Carbohydrate** 15g
**Fiber** 1g
**Total Fat** 4g
**Saturated Fat** 1g
**Cholesterol** 0mg
**Sodium** 234mg

ORGANIC
BLUE AGAVE

# Almonds

Sprinkled on top or baked inside, almonds add unique flavor and texture to many dishes, savory or sweet. And is there any other snack that's as delicious and satisfying as a handful of high-protein, high-fiber almonds?

## benefits

Almonds are one of the healthiest tree nuts. They provide calcium, fiber, vitamin E, magnesium, B vitamins and more. One fourth of a cup of almonds contains more protein than a typical egg! Better yet, almonds are packed with flavor as well and even a sprinkling of nuts can make a vegan vegetable dish a lot more satisfying. Like all nuts, almonds are high in fat, but most of it is the heart-healthy monounsaturated kind.

## selection and storage

Almonds can be purchased in the shell, raw, dry- or oil-roasted, sliced, blanched, slivered, salted, smoked or flavored. They are quite perishable, so purchase from a store with a high turnover so you know they haven't been on the shelf long. Almonds stay fresh only two to four weeks in the pantry. If you won't use them right away, store almonds in your freezer where they will last for up to a year. If they develop an off odor or rancid flavor, it's time to toss them.

## preparation

Toasting almonds adds to their flavor and crunch. You can toast in a dry skillet over medium heat, shaking the nuts often. They're done once they begin to color and become fragrant (about 5 minutes for sliced almonds). Remove them immediately as they can burn in a matter of seconds. To toast in the oven, preheat to 350°F and spread the nuts on a baking sheet. Bake 10 to 15 minutes, stirring occasionally.

## recipe suggestions

Sliced almonds are an excellent topper for just about any vegetable dish. Use almonds in place of cheese to add richness to pasta dishes or casseroles. Homemade almond butter is easy with a food processor. Process nuts for 10 to 20 minutes. Be patient. First the nuts will form crumbs, then a paste and then they will smooth out as oil is released. Add salt, agave or other flavorings if you like.

# caribbean sweet potato and bean stew

2 medium sweet potatoes (about
   1 pound), peeled and cut into
   1-inch cubes
2 cups frozen cut green beans
1 can (about 15 ounces) black beans,
   rinsed and drained
1 can (about 14 ounces) vegetable broth
1 small onion, sliced
2 teaspoons Caribbean jerk seasoning
½ teaspoon dried thyme
¼ teaspoon salt
¼ teaspoon ground cinnamon
⅓ cup slivered almonds, toasted
   Hot pepper sauce (optional)

**Slow Cooker Directions**

1. Combine sweet potatoes, green beans, black beans, broth, onion, seasoning, thyme, salt and cinnamon in slow cooker. Cover; cook on LOW 5 to 6 hours or until vegetables are tender.

2. Serve with almonds and hot pepper sauce.

*Makes 4 servings*

## nutrients per serving:

**Calories** 196
**Calories from Fat** 1%
**Protein** 0g

**Carbohydrate** 44g
**Fiber** 11g
**Total Fat** <1g
**Saturated Fat** 0g
**Cholesterol** 0mg
**Sodium** 124mg

# Artichokes

The artichoke's spiky exterior hides a soft heart. Their delicate flavor and smooth meaty texture will enrich everything from dips to pasta. And what other vegetable is such mysterious fun to eat!

## benefits

Enjoy fresh artichokes as a healthy appetizer. They're high in fiber and folate and low in calories. Artichoke hearts are available canned (marinated or in water) and frozen, so they make convenient additions to casseroles, salads and pasta courses. Their rich flavor and dense texture make vegan dishes more filling and substantial.

## selection and storage

Peak season for fresh artichokes is the spring. Look for baby artichokes as well as the giant globe artichoke. Baby artichokes are not really babies; they grow on the sides of the plant's stem. A fresh artichoke's petals should be tightly closed and it should be heavy for its size. Store fresh artichokes in the refrigerator, wrapped with a damp paper towel to prevent drying. Flavor is best if you use them within a few days, but they will keep at least a week if properly stored.

## preparation

Whole artichokes can be boiled, steamed, pressure cooked or even microwaved. Trim the stem and snap off the dark outer leaves until you reach those that are paler green. Cut off the bristly tips of the leaves with knife or scissors. The simple way to remove the choke, which is the fuzzy purplish cone deep inside, is to cut the artichoke in half so it's easier to see the choke. Scoop it out with a melon baller or grapefruit spoon. Baby artichokes are much easier to handle since their chokes are usually not developed. Just remove dried outer leaves and other prickly parts. All artichokes discolor once cut surfaces are exposed to air. To lessen darkening, keep them in water with a squeeze of lemon juice.

## recipe suggestions

Artichoke hearts make an excellent hot or cold dip blended with vegan mayonnaise and seasonings. Whole artichokes make a dramatic first course and can be served with lemon-flavored olive oil for dipping. Mediterranean cooks pair artichokes with mushrooms, olives and walnuts. Baby artichokes can be sautéed and served as a side dish.

# vegan artichoke lasagna

- 1 tablespoon olive oil
- 1 cup chopped sweet onion
- 3 cloves garlic, chopped (2 tablespoons)
- ¼ cup tomato paste
- ¼ cup white wine
- 1 can (28 ounces) Italian plum tomatoes, undrained, or crushed tomatoes
- 1 teaspoon dried oregano
- 3 teaspoons kosher salt, divided
- 2 teaspoons sugar, divided
- 9 uncooked lasagna noodles
- 1 package (14 ounces) firm tofu, pressed
- 1 cup silken tofu
- ½ cup chopped parsley
- 2 teaspoons lemon juice
- 1 teaspoon black pepper
- 1 can (14 ounces) artichoke hearts, drained and chopped
- 1 package (10 ounces) chopped frozen spinach, thawed and squeezed dry
- 8 ounces dairy-free mozzarella cheese alternative, shredded
- 2 roasted bell peppers, chopped

**1.** For sauce, heat oil in large saucepan over medium-high heat. Add onion and garlic; cook and stir 5 minutes or until onion is tender. Stir in tomato paste; cook 1 minute. Stir in wine; cook 30 seconds. Add tomatoes with juice, oregano, 1 teaspoon salt and 1 teaspoon sugar; break up tomatoes with spoon. Reduce heat; cover and simmer 30 minutes.

**2.** Prepare lasagna noodles according to package directions. Drain and return to saucepan; cover with cold water to prevent sticking.

**3** Crumble firm tofu into large bowl. Add silken tofu, parsley, lemon juice, black pepper and remaining 2 teaspoons salt and 1 teaspoon sugar; mix well. Combine artichokes and spinach in small bowl.

**4.** Preheat oven to 350°F. Grease 13×9-inch baking dish. Spread ½ cup sauce in dish; lay 3 noodles over sauce. Spread half of tofu mixture over noodles; top with artichoke mixture, half of shredded mozzarella alternative and ½ cup sauce. Repeat layers of noodles and tofu; top with bell peppers, remaining 3 noodles, sauce and mozzarella alternative. Cover with greased foil.

**5.** Bake 45 minutes. Remove foil; bake 15 minutes. Let stand 10 minutes before cutting into squares.          *Makes 8 servings*

# Arugula

Arugula's sharp, peppery flavor is a trendy addition to salads, but it's been cultivated since Roman times when it was considered an aphrodisiac. Arugula adds zip and good nutrition to soups, sauces and pasta dishes, too.

## benefits

Arugula, which is also called rocket or rucola, is related to kale, broccoli and other cruciferous vegetables. It is high in vitamin A, vitamin C, vitamin K, folate and calcium. That's in addition to being a rich source of phytonutrients that can help naturally detoxify the body. Arugula is much more versatile than most salad greens. It can be used instead of, or in addition to, spinach to boost flavor in a stir-fry or added at the last minute to wilt into a soup or pasta dish to increase the nutrients.

## selection and storage

You'll find arugula year-round in supermarkets. It's part of most mesclun salad mixes and is also sold in bunches, sometimes with the roots attached. Baby arugula tends to have a milder flavor than the larger leaves, which can sometimes be quite spicy. Refrigerate arugula in a sealed bag before washing and use it within a few days. Arugula is easy to grow even in a window garden and it's a cut-and-come-again green that keeps on producing even after leaves have been harvested.

## preparation

Virtually the only prep required for arugula is a thorough washing. Grit and dirt tend to get stuck on the tender leaves. Give it a gentle dunk right before you're ready to use it as it bruises easily. If you do need to clean arugula ahead of time, spread the cleaned leaves on paper towels, roll them up and refrigerate loosely wrapped.

## recipe suggestions

Pesto made from arugula and basil or parsley is delicious. Arugula is traditional in all sorts of salads, and pairs especially well with tomatoes and avocados. Line a plate with arugula and top it with a grain dish like tabbouleh. Stir it into beans or rice to add color and interest. In a sandwich, arugula beats lettuce for flavor and nutrition hands down. Or try the healthy Egyptian breakfast of arugula mixed with beans, olive oil and parsley.

**nutrients per serving:**

**Calories** 221

**Calories from Fat** 17%
**Protein** 7g
**Carbohydrate** 38g
**Fiber** 7g

**Total Fat** 4g
**Saturated Fat** 1g
**Cholesterol** 0mg
**Sodium** 146mg

# rigatoni salad

12 ounces rigatoni pasta, cooked and
  drained
1 to 2 cups chopped arugula
1 package (10 ounces) frozen snow peas
  or sugar snap peas, thawed
8 ounces cherry tomatoes, cut into halves
1 medium red or yellow bell pepper, cut
  into thin strips
½ red onion, cut into thin strips
⅓ cup sliced black olives
⅓ to ½ cup Italian vinaigrette

Combine all ingredients in large serving bowl;
toss gently.          *Makes about 8 servings*

**Note:** Vary the amounts of each ingredient
according to your taste. Substitute steamed
green beans (whole or cut) for the peas or
add steamed, sliced carrots, zucchini or
yellow squash.

# Asian Noodles

Thick or thin, curly or flat, made of wheat, rice and even buckwheat, Asian noodles offer a continent's worth of flavors and textures to explore. Next time you want to turn vegetables into a meal, just start noodling around.

## benefits

Asian noodles offer such variety and versatility you'll never tire of them. While some, like Cantonese egg noodles, aren't vegan, most are. Check the ingredient lists to be sure. For a change of pace, try the hearty Japanese buckwheat noodles called soba. Rice noodles or cellophane noodles are perfect for vegans who are also avoiding gluten.

## selection and storage

For a mind-boggling selection of noodles, visit an Asian market. Chinese mein noodles (the kind in chow mein) are wheat noodles similar to pasta and a great all-purpose choice. They are sold in neat bundles or curled into nests. If wheat noodles have a golden color, they may contain eggs, so beware. Soba buckwheat noodles are beige to dark brown. Japanese somen and udon are both wheat noodles. Somen are thinner and sometimes colored with green tea. Thicker udon noodles are often served in soups. Ramen, that staple of college dorms that come with a seasoning packet, are fried before being dried. The noodles are usually vegan friendly, but the seasoning packets may include animal products. Rice noodles are delightfully slippery and come in a range of widths. Cellophane noodles look like a bunch of tangled little nests usually packed in a plastic fishnet-type bag. They are made of bean flour and work for both vegan and gluten-free diets.

## preparation

Like pasta, wheat noodles should usually be cooked in a large pot of boiling water. Consult the directions for the individual variety and check doneness before the suggested time. Rice noodles and cellophane noodles only need to be soaked in warm or hot water until they soften.

## recipe suggestions

Noodles are flavor sponges, perfect for serving under a saucy stir-fry or skillet dish. Think of them as multipurpose side dishes, not just part of Asian recipes. Soba noodles are excellent in a cold salad, and a simple dish of Chinese wheat noodles flavored with ginger, green onion and garlic pairs well with grilled tofu.

# szechuan vegetable lo mein

- 2 cans (about 14 ounces each) vegetable broth
- 2 teaspoons minced garlic
- 1 teaspoon minced fresh ginger
- ¼ teaspoon red pepper flakes
- 1 package (16 ounces) frozen mixed vegetables
- 1 package (5 ounces) Asian curly noodles
- 3 tablespoons soy sauce
- 1 tablespoon dark sesame oil
- ¼ cup thinly sliced green onions

1. Combine broth, garlic, ginger and red pepper flakes in large deep skillet. Cover and bring to a boil over high heat.

2. Add vegetables and noodles to skillet; cover and return to a boil. Reduce heat to medium-low; simmer, uncovered, 5 to 6 minutes or until vegetables and noodles are tender, stirring occasionally.

3. Stir in soy sauce and sesame oil; cook 3 minutes. Stir in green onions; ladle into bowls.  *Makes 4 servings*

Note: For a heartier, protein-packed main dish, add 1 package (14 ounces) extra firm tofu, drained and cut into ¾-inch pieces, to the broth mixture with the soy sauce and sesame oil.

## nutrients per serving:

**Calories** 225
**Calories from Fat** 15%
**Protein** 4g
**Carbohydrate** 42g
**Fiber** 3g
**Total Fat** 3g
**Saturated Fat** 4g
**Cholesterol** 0mg
**Sodium** 1,257mg

# Asparagus

Tall, slender asparagus is one of nature's most beautiful vegetables. How fortunate that it's also delicious and nutritious. Finger food, main dish, soup, salad or side—about the only place asparagus doesn't belong is dessert.

## benefits

Asparagus has a well-balanced nutritional profile, providing vitamins A and C, plus B vitamins, antioxidants, folate and fiber. Since ancient times it's been valued both as a vegetable and a health food. Greeks and Romans enjoyed it fresh and also dried it for winter use.

## selection and storage

Asparagus is a welcome sign of spring, so celebrate the season by enjoying fresh, locally grown shoots when they are at their best and least expensive. Most asparagus grown in the U.S. is green, though a delectable purple variety is now showing up in farmers' markets and some produce departments. Whatever the color or size, look for stalks that have tightly closed tips and smooth straight stalks. Thickness is not an indicator of age or quality. In fact, thick and thin can even come from the same plant! Choose whichever will work better in your recipe. Asparagus is very perishable. Refrigerate it with the ends wrapped in a damp paper towel, or placed upright in a glass with an inch of water in the bottom.

## preparation

The bottom of an asparagus spear can be tough and woody. Snap it off and it will usually break in the right place. Should you peel asparagus? No need to peel thin stalks. Thick ones benefit from using a potato peeler to take off a bit of the tough outer layer of skin. That way the asparagus can be cooked until crisp-tender without overcooking to get the skin soft. You can boil, steam or microwave asparagus. Just be careful not to overcook it or it becomes drab and stringy. Try roasting or grilling the spears for a deeper flavor.

## recipe suggestions

The skinniest asparagus can be enjoyed raw and works well in a salad. As a side dish, try serving asparagus with a vinaigrette or vegan mayonnaise and toasted bread crumbs. Asparagus is perfect in pasta dishes, grain-based main courses, stir-fries and rice dishes. The flavor marries well with mushrooms, bell peppers, tomatoes, peas and potatoes.

# bulgur with asparagus and spring herbs

⅔ cup uncooked bulgur wheat*
2 cups sliced asparagus (1-inch pieces)
½ cup frozen peas, thawed
⅔ cup chopped fresh Italian parsley
2 teaspoons finely chopped fresh mint
3 tablespoons lemon juice
1 tablespoon orange juice
1 tablespoon extra-virgin olive oil
⅛ teaspoon salt
⅛ teaspoon black pepper

*Bulgur is a whole grain that's high in fiber and protein. See page 42 for more information.

1. Prepare bulgur according to package directions. Drain well.

2. Steam asparagus in steamer basket 3 to 4 minutes or until bright green and crisp-tender. Rinse under cold running water to cool and blot dry with paper towels.

3. Combine bulgur, asparagus, peas, parsley and mint in large bowl. Whisk lemon juice, orange juice, oil, salt and pepper in small bowl. Pour over salad; toss gently.

*Makes 4 servings*

## nutrients per serving:

**Calories** 148

**Calories from Fat** 24%
**Protein** 6g
**Carbohydrate** 25g
**Fiber** 7g

**Total Fat** 4g
**Saturated Fat** 1g
**Cholesterol** 0mg
**Sodium** 98mg

# Avocado

Avocado is a fruit that is often used as a vegetable. It's a salad ingredient that can also be a dessert. Delectable uses for this rich, creamy textured fruit are as limitless as your imagination.

## benefits

Avocados taste luxurious. Part of the reason is that they are high in fat. Unlike animal products, though, the fat in an avocado is monounsaturated— that's the good kind that can actually help lower cholesterol. They also contribute nearly 20 different types of vitamins, minerals and phytonutrients. One of the many delights of the avocado is that its buttery texture and creamy flavor make it a natural substitute for dairy in smoothies, sauces, soups and salsas.

## selection and storage

The two most common types of avocados are the pebbly-skinned, dark green Haas, and the smoother skinned, light green Florida avocado. Fruit should be heavy for its size. The Haas variety is dark blackish green when ripe; other varieties may stay a paler green. Avocados ripen after they've been picked, so if you're not using them at once choose those that are still firm. Ripen at room temperature until the fruit yields to gentle pressure. To speed things up, place the avocado in a paper bag with an apple. Once ripe you can refrigerate an avocado for a day or two.

## preparation

To peel an avocado, cut it lengthwise around the seed. Twist the two haves until they separate. Spoon underneath the seed and lift it out. Then you can easily peel off the skin with fingers or knife or just scoop out the flesh. Keep lemon or lime juice handy to sprinkle on the cut surfaces, preventing the discoloration that happens when the avocado flesh is exposed to the air. Contrary to popular belief, burying the pit in the mashed avocado won't help!

## recipe suggestions

Use avocado as a sandwich spread in place of butter or mayo. Add slices to salads or dice to use as a garnish on soups or main courses. It's not a good idea to cook an avocado as it can become bitter. Add it to hot pasta or grain dishes at the last minute just until heated. Oh, and don't forget the guacamole!

# Balsamic Vinegar

It's hard to believe that one condiment can add such depth of flavor to so many things. Balsamic vinegar has been revered as an ingredient and a healing tonic in Italy for more than a century. Its sweet-tart richness belongs in your pantry.

## benefits

The word "balsamic" comes from the same root as "balm." Hundreds of years ago Italians considered balsamic to be a pain reliever, healthy tonic and even a cure for the plague. It was so valuable, it was sometimes presented to royalty as a gift. The balsamic we use today is a more humble condiment, but it still has the power to transform a simple tomato or eggplant into a different kind of delicious.

## selection and storage

Authentic Aceto Balsamico di Modena comes only from the Modena region of Italy and is strictly regulated. The distinctive flavor results from 12 years of aging in different wooden barrels. For obvious reasons this balsamic is quite expensive and can cost $100 a bottle!

Fortunately, there are many affordable and delicious alternatives. Look for an Italian balsamic vinegar that has been aged at least three years. Price is one indicator of quality—that huge jug may be cheap, but it won't taste very good. Check the ingredient lists as well. Some balsamic has sugar or artificial color added to make it look like the real thing. In a cool, dark cupboard, balsamic vinegar should last for about three years.

## preparation

To use balsamic as a drizzle over vegetables or fruit, you may want to reduce it to thicken it and concentrate the flavor. Pour about four times as much as you'll need into a small pan. Bring the vinegar to a simmer and cook until it reaches a syrupy consistency. Watch carefully and lower the heat if it begins to scorch. Turn on the fan over the stove or open a window since the fumes can be quite strong.

## recipe suggestions

Use balsamic vinegar to make an easy vinaigrette that beats any bottled dressing. Combine one part balsamic with two parts extra virgin olive oil in a jar. Add salt, pepper and Italian seasoning; cover and shake to combine. A drizzle of balsamic brings out the sweetness of garden tomatoes or strawberries. Try a bit over roasted vegetables or on a fruit salad. Balsamic also adds depth and richness to pan sauces or marinades.

# Bananas

Sunny yellow bananas add tropical sweetness to cooking and snacking. They even come in their own handy, easy-open package. Great nutrition and amazing versatility make bananas a super food.

## benefits

Bananas are a good source of potassium, fiber, vitamin C and vitamin $B_6$. Since many of the best sources of $B_6$, other than fortified cereals, are meat or fish, bananas can be an important contributor to vegan nutrition. In addition, bananas can be mashed or puréed to add creaminess to many dishes without adding dairy products.

## selection and storage

There are many types of bananas, including red bananas and baby bananas, but the most familiar is the yellow Cavendish. Bananas ripen after picking, and as they do, their starch turns to sugar. Bananas will ripen at room temperature in a day or two. To speed things up, place them in a brown paper bag with an apple, or store them someplace warm, like near the oven. Every stage of ripeness has its uses. Green bananas, like their close cousin the plantain, can be prepared almost like a vegetable in stews or other savory dishes. Overripe bananas work well in baked goods. Freeze chunks of ripe bananas to use in smoothies or banana bread and use them within a month or two.

## preparation

Peeling is all the preparation bananas require. For fun, try peeling from the non-stem end. That's how monkeys do it and it's usually easier. On the plant, banana bunches actually face upwards, rather than hanging down, so you'll be peeling from the top of the fruit! To prevent banana slices from browning once cut, brush them with a bit of lemon juice.

## recipe suggestions

Bananas work for breakfast, lunch or dinner. Try mashed bananas as a spread for your morning bagel or add slices to your peanut butter sandwich. Add them to a spinach or fruit salad. Turn bananas into a chutney or a relish. Paired with melon, pineapple, mango or coconut they can be an appetizer or dessert. Smoothies made with frozen bananas are extra thick and creamy. And don't forget banana bread, banana pudding and chocolate covered bananas. There are never ending ways to go bananas!

# Barley

Barley has a nutty flavor and slightly chewy texture that make it a satisfying addition to soups, salads, casseroles and stews. Try barley for a nutritious, delicious change from rice or pasta.

## benefits

Barley is a high fiber food and contains the same cholesterol-lowering soluble fiber (beta-glucan) that is found in oat bran. It also provides selenium, a trace mineral that is needed daily to support metabolism and immune function. Whole grains are an important part of any healthy diet and barley is one of the best. It's a shame that it is often overlooked since it can play most of the same roles as wheat or rice.

## selection and storage

Hulled (whole grain) barley has only its outer husk removed, so it's the most nutritious form. It does require more soaking and cooking time. Pearl barley is the most commonly available and quickest cooking. Part of the bran and endosperm layer are removed during the polishing process, therefore pearl barley is not considered a whole grain. It is lower in fiber and nutrients, but pearl barley is still quite nutritious. Scotch barley falls halfway between hulled barley and pearl barley in terms of processing as well as nutritional benefits. Purchase barley from a market where there is a high turnover to guarantee freshness and store it in an airtight container in a cool, dark, dry place.

## preparation

Regular pearl barley needs to be cooked in boiling water for 45 to 60 minutes. Hulled (whole grain) barley takes 60 to 90 minutes to cook. Soaking the grains overnight first will reduce cooking time. To save time, prepare extra barley and freeze it in one-cup portions in freezer bags, where it will keep for up to three months. Defrost the cooked barley in your microwave as you need it.

## recipe suggestions

Barley is delicious in soup, but that's just a start. In casseroles or stews, barley adds heartiness and a nutty flavor. It makes an excellent pilaf and can also be prepared risotto style. Use barley to stuff tomatoes, mushrooms or squash. Add it to fruit salads to make them more nutritious and satisfying. Barley flour is a great addition to waffles, pancakes or breads and barley flakes can be added to other cereals or enjoyed on their own.

# Basil

The sweet, spicy fragrance of fresh basil can transport you to a summer day on the Mediterranean. For thousands of years, basil was considered a royal or holy herb, filled with magical properties.

## benefits

We no longer believe basil will cure the bite of a dragon as they did in ancient Greece, but basil is rich in antioxidants that can protect the body's cells from damage that can lead to disease. Basil's volatile oils have proven antibacterial and anti-inflammatory properties, too, so maybe the Greeks were on to something. Best of all, basil can brighten a dull dish or make a simple plate of pasta sing.

## selection and storage

Sweet or Genovese basil is the most common variety, but there are countless others, including anise-flavored Thai basil, lemon basil, cinnamon basil and opal basil, which is deep purple. Whichever kind you choose—and why not try them all—use it as soon as possible. To store it, try trimming the stem ends and arranging them in a jar or glass of water like a bouquet. Cover the leaves loosely with a plastic bag, and keep it out of direct sun in a cool place. The basil should last for several days. (In fact, if you see roots developing, replant the basil in a pot or in your garden.) Basil can also be very successfully frozen. Purée the leaves with a bit of water or oil and freeze in an ice cube tray so you can use small portions as needed.

## preparation

Pesto is the classic basil preparation. See the recipe opposite for a delicious vegan version. Remove any large, tough stems before measuring or using basil leaves. If you don't have a food processor, or you want to do it the way an Italian grandma would, you can use a mortar and pestle. Fresh basil should usually be added at the very end of a recipe since the fresh flavor is lost in long cooking.

## recipe suggestions

Of course Italian cooking calls out for basil, but think beyond pasta. Thai and other Asian noodle dishes often make good use of basil. Try sprinkling slivered basil leaves over fresh oranges or strawberries or adding it to sautéed vegetables.

# vegan pesto

- 1 pound uncooked whole wheat fettuccine
- 1 cup packed fresh basil leaves
- ½ cup pine nuts, toasted*
- 2 cloves garlic
- ½ teaspoon salt
- ¼ teaspoon black pepper
- ¼ cup plus 1 tablespoon olive oil, divided

*To toast pine nuts, spread in a single layer in heavy skillet. Cook over low heat 1 to 2 minutes or until nuts are lightly browned, stirring frequently.*

1. Bring large saucepan of water to a boil. Add pasta; cook according to package directions. Drain; set aside and keep warm.

2. Meanwhile, place basil, pine nuts, garlic, salt and pepper in food processor; drizzle with 1 tablespoon olive oil. Process about 10 seconds or until coarsely chopped. With motor running, drizzle in remaining ¼ cup olive oil. Process about 30 seconds or until almost smooth. Toss with hot cooked pasta.          *Makes 4 servings*

Note: Pesto can be made 1 week in advance. Store in airtight container in the refrigerator. Makes ½ cup pesto.

## nutrients per serving:

**Calories** 690

**Calories from Fat** 40%
**Protein** 17g
**Carbohydrate** 87g
**Fiber** 5g

**Total Fat** 31g
**Saturated Fat** 3g
**Cholesterol** 0mg
**Sodium** 342mg

# Beets

You can't beat beets for sweetness, color and nutrition. Their unique, earthy flavor is wonderful on its own or as part of a soup, salad or main course.

## benefits

Beets have good looks and good nutrition. The bright color indicates the presence of a unique mix of phytonutrients that can neutralize toxins in our bodies and protect against disease. If that weren't enough, beets are also high in potassium and fiber and low in calories. As part of a plant-based diet they offer versatility and a smooth, dense texture many vegetables lack.

## selection and storage

The best beets are fresh beets. While red beets are standard, in season look for mellow yellow beets or the gorgeous Chioggia, which have a candy-striped interior. Beets should be firm and heavy for their size. Seeing the greens attached is an excellent indicator of freshness and a bonus. The greens cook beautifully and taste a lot like chard, which is a close relative. Separate the greens from the beets before refrigerating them or the greens will continue to take moisture from the root causing it to shrivel. Tightly wrapped, beets will last several weeks in the refrigerator. Beet greens remain fresh only a few days. Look for packaged, precooked beets in the refrigerated part of some produce departments. Canned beets and pickled beets are two other options.

## preparation

The easiest way to cook beets and keep your hands relatively unstained is to roast them. Leave about an inch of stem attached, scrub gently, wrap in foil and place in a baking pan. Average size beets take about an hour at 400°F. Cooking times vary with size, age and variety. Poke through the foil with a fork to see if they're done. Beets can also be steamed, microwaved, boiled or sautéed. Wear kitchen gloves and an apron to avoid staining.

## recipe suggestions

The sweetness of beets pairs well with citrus and other acidic ingredients. Keep roasted beets in the refrigerator and you'll have an easy addition to a grain-based main course. You can thinly slice raw beets and fry them for tasty chips. Grated raw beets are a nice addition to a salad or a slaw.

## nutrients per serving:

**Calories** 100
**Calories from Fat** 20%
**Protein** 2g

**Carbohydrate** 19g
**Fiber** 2g
**Total Fat** 3g

**Saturated Fat** 0g
**Cholesterol** 0mg
**Sodium** 100mg

# orange and maple glazed roasted beets

- 4 medium beets, scrubbed
- 2 teaspoons olive oil
- 2 teaspoons grated orange peel, divided
- ¼ cup orange juice
- 3 tablespoons balsamic or cider vinegar
- 2 tablespoons maple syrup
- 1 teaspoon Dijon mustard
- 1 to 2 tablespoons chopped fresh mint (optional)
  Salt and black pepper

1. Preheat oven to 425°F.

2. Rub beets with oil; place in baking dish. Cover and bake 45 minutes to 1 hour or until knife inserted into largest beet goes in easily. Let stand until cool.

3. Peel and cut in half lengthwise; cut into wedges. Return beets to baking dish.

4. Whisk 1 teaspoon orange peel, orange juice, vinegar, maple syrup and mustard in small bowl until blended. Pour over beets.

5. Bake 10 to 15 minutes or until heated through and marinade is absorbed. Sprinkle with remaining 1 teaspoon orange peel and mint, if desired. Season with salt and pepper.

*Makes 4 servings*

# Bell Peppers

Bell peppers come in a rainbow of colors and flavors. Green bell peppers taste fresh and herbal. Red peppers can be amazingly sweet. Yellow and orange bells are fruity and all of them are delightfully crunchy.

## benefits

A red bell pepper has more vitamin C than a typical orange. All bell peppers, also called sweet peppers, are good sources of vitamin A, potassium and antioxidants, including lutein, which helps protect sight. Bell peppers make important contributions to a plant-based diet by providing flavor, color and crunch without adding fat or a lot of calories.

## selection and storage

Pick peppers that are glossy and brightly colored. Stems should be fresh looking, not shriveled, and the peppers should feel firm with no soft spots or cracks. All bell peppers start out green and depending on the variety they ripen into red, orange, yellow, purple or brown. Store bell peppers, unwashed, in a plastic bag in the refrigerator's crisper drawer. Green peppers will last for up to a week; other colors are more perishable. You can freeze chopped bell peppers for up to six months, although they lose crispness once thawed.

## preparation

Wash peppers to remove the wax coating. Cut the pepper around the stem and pull out the membrane and seeds along with the stem. Roasting peppers brings out a different flavor. You can roast by holding a whole pepper over a gas flame with a long handled fork until the skin browns and blisters. Place it in a paper bag for about 10 minutes to steam and loosen the skin. Then peel off the outer skin and remove the stem, membrane and seeds. In a broiler, place halves of peppers skin side up on a baking sheet. Broil for 5 to 10 minutes until the skin is blistered.

## recipe suggestions

Enjoy bell peppers raw with a dip or in a salad. Bell pepper strips add color and a touch of sweetness to stir-fries and sautés of all kinds. Whole bell peppers make gorgeous containers for serving dips and can also be stuffed with rice and other grains. Roasted red bell peppers make an excellent spread or sauce when puréed with garlic, herbs and a bit of olive oil.

# four-pepper black bean fajitas

- 3 tablespoons olive oil, divided
- 3 medium bell peppers, cut into strips
- 2 medium onions, cut into ¼-inch wedges
- 1 can (about 15 ounces) black beans, rinsed and drained
- ¼ cup water
- 2 tablespoons lime juice
- 1 canned chipotle pepper in adobo sauce
- 1 clove garlic, minced
- ¼ teaspoon salt
- 8 (8-inch) flour tortillas
- ¼ cup chopped fresh cilantro
  Lime wedges (optional)

1. Heat 1 tablespoon oil in large skillet over medium-high heat. Add bell peppers and onions; cook and stir 12 minutes or until beginning to brown.

2. Meanwhile, combine beans, water, remaining 2 tablespoons oil, lime juice, chipotle, garlic and salt in food processor or blender; process until smooth. Place in medium microwavable bowl. Cover with plastic wrap. Microwave on HIGH 2 to 3 minutes or until heated through. Heat tortillas according to package directions.

3. To serve, divide bean mixture among tortillas; top with bell pepper mixture. Sprinkle with cilantro and serve with lime wedges.

*Makes 4 servings*

## nutrients per serving:

**Calories** 508
**Calories from Fat** 31%
**Protein** 16g
**Carbohydrate** 74g
**Fiber** 10g

**Total Fat** 18g
**Saturated Fat** 3g
**Cholesterol** 0mg
**Sodium** 1,082mg

# Black Beans

Beautiful, beneficial black beans are an important part of the vegan diet. Favorites in Mexican and Mediterranean cuisines, black beans are versatile and full of flavor. Enjoy them in soups, salads, with grains or rice, even in brownies!

## benefits

Like other legumes, black beans, sometimes called turtle beans, are good sources of protein, fiber, iron, calcium, zinc and B vitamins. A single one-cup serving of black beans provides nearly 15 grams of fiber—that's over half the recommended daily value. The creamy texture, meaty flavor and high protein make black beans the perfect ingredient for a satisfying vegan meal.

## selection and storage

Even dried black beans have a shelf life. While they may not spoil, old beans become hard, lose flavor and take longer to cook. Buy dried black beans from a market that gets high turnover. Ethnic markets featuring Mexican or Latin foods offer many brands of beans at bargain prices. Packaged or from a bulk bin, dried black beans should show no evidence of moisture and should not be dusty or cracked. Store them in a cool, dry, dark place in an airtight container for up to a year. Canned black beans are a great option to have in your cupboard and are nutritionally very close to dried beans you cook yourself.

## preparation

To cook dried black beans, first rinse and sort them. Check for small stones or damaged beans and discard them. Presoaking makes beans easier to digest and shortens cooking time. For a quick soaking method, see the recipe on the facing page. If you have more time, you can soak the beans for 8 hours or overnight. Make more dried beans than you need and freeze the rest in small bags or containers for later use. If you are using canned black beans, rinse and drain them to eliminate some of the salt.

## recipe suggestions

Black beans work well as a filling for tacos, quesadillas, burritos or anything else Mexican. Include some in salads, especially grain-based ones. Add a sprinkling of black beans to a pizza topping. Black bean burgers are a tasty vegetarian option. Bean purées can even replace some fat in baked goods.

# black bean chili

- 1 pound uncooked dried black beans
- 6 cups water
- 1 bay leaf
- 3 tablespoons vegetable oil
- 2 large onions, chopped
- 3 cloves garlic, minced
- 1 can (14½ ounces) whole tomatoes, undrained
- 2 to 3 jalapeño peppers, seeded and minced
- 2 tablespoons chili powder
- 1½ teaspoons salt
- 1 teaspoon paprika
- 1 teaspoon dried oregano
- 1 teaspoon unsweetened cocoa powder
- ½ teaspoon ground cumin
- ¼ teaspoon ground cinnamon
- 1 tablespoon red wine vinegar
  Sliced green onions

1. Rinse and sort beans, discarding any broken beans or foreign matter. Place in 8-quart Dutch oven and cover with cold water by 2 inches. Cover; bring to a boil over high heat. Boil 2 minutes. Remove from heat; let soak, covered, 1 hour.

2. Drain beans. Add 6 cups water and bay leaf. Bring to a boil. Reduce heat and simmer, partially covered, 1 to 2 hours or until tender.

3. Meanwhile, heat oil in large skillet over medium heat. Add onions and garlic; cook until onions are tender. Coarsely chop tomatoes; add to skillet with juice. Add jalapeño peppers, chili powder, salt, paprika, oregano, cocoa powder, cumin and cinnamon. Simmer 15 minutes. Add tomato mixture and vinegar to beans. Simmer until chili has thickened slightly. Discard bay leaf. Sprinkle with green onions.

*Makes 6 servings*

## nutrients per serving:

**Calories** 360
**Calories from Fat** 21%
**Protein** 18g
**Carbohydrate** 56g
**Fiber** 15g
**Total Fat** 9g
**Saturated Fat** 1g
**Cholesterol** 0mg
**Sodium** 851mg

# Blueberries

Enjoy blueberries at breakfast, lunch or dinner. Research keeps finding more health benefits for these tiny nutritional powerhouses, but their tart sweet taste is reason enough to enjoy them more often.

## benefits

Would you like to fight free radicals? Want to improve your memory? Get your vitamin C? Blueberries can help with all that and more. They are antioxidant superstars, ranking near the top among antioxidant foods. Native Americans gathered this native wild fruit to eat and use for medicinal purposes. How fortunate that blueberries are now readily available year round fresh, frozen or dried.

## selection and storage

Blueberries are in season from May through October and are at their sweetest

and best when freshly picked. Sort through the berries, removing pieces of stem and discarding any shriveled berries. Don't wash them until you're ready to use them since moisture makes them spoil more quickly. Luckily blueberries freeze very well, so stock up when they are plentiful. To preserve the harvest, spread berries in a single layer on a rimmed baking sheet. Once frozen solid, berries can be transferred to plastic freezer bags and will keep for at least six months. Wild blueberries are often available frozen. They are a bit smaller than the cultivated berry and even higher in antioxidants.

## preparation

When adding blueberries to pancakes or other baked goods be aware that their color can bleed. To minimize the effect, make sure the berries are dry, add them at the last minute and mix gently. You can arrange them individually by pushing them into the top of a pancake while the bottom is cooking. If they are frozen, don't thaw them first. If you've ever made baked goods containing blueberries that turned greenish-brown, the culprit is most likely baking soda, which is alkaline. See if you can adjust the recipe to use baking powder instead.

## recipe suggestions

It's hard to beat blueberry muffins or blueberry pancakes for breakfast, but try blueberries in smoothies, too. Add frozen blueberries to oatmeal or other hot cereals; they'll thaw in minutes. Blueberries work well in fruit or grain salads and can be turned into a sauce to serve with sweet or savory dishes. Dried blueberries can be added to trail mix or cereal bars.

## blueberry poppy seed coffee cake

¾ cup soymilk or other dairy-free milk
1 tablespoon lemon juice or vinegar
1½ cups all-purpose flour
½ cup sugar
1 teaspoon baking powder
½ teaspoon baking soda
¼ teaspoon salt
¼ cup (½ stick) cold dairy-free margarine, cut into small pieces
1 tablespoon poppy seeds
Prepared egg replacer equal to 1 egg
1 teaspoon vanilla
1 teaspoon grated lemon peel
1 cup fresh blueberries

1. Preheat oven to 350°F. Spray 9-inch round pan with nonstick cooking spray. Combine soymilk and lemon juice in measuring cup. Let stand 5 minutes to sour.

2. Combine flour, sugar, baking powder, baking soda and salt in large bowl. Cut in margarine with pastry blender or two knives until mixture resembles coarse crumbs. Stir in poppy seeds.

3. Whisk soured soymilk, egg replacer, vanilla and lemon peel in small bowl until blended. Stir soymilk mixture into flour mixture just until moistened. Spread half of batter into prepared pan; top with blueberries. Drop remaining batter in 8 dollops onto blueberries.

4. Bake 33 to 36 minutes or until top is golden brown. Cool 15 minutes in pan on wire rack. Serve warm. *Makes 8 servings*

# Bok Choy

Bok choy, or pak choy, is also called Chinese cabbage and comes in dozens of shapes and sizes. All varieties have a mild, slightly sweet flavor and delicate crunch that is easy to love.

## benefits

Bok choy is a low calorie, zero fat food that has tons of vitamin A, vitamin C, vitamin K and vitamin $B_6$. In fact, one cup of shredded bok choy will more than fill your daily requirement for vitamin A. Like all members of the cabbage family, bok choy is also a good source of fiber and is rich in antioxidants. With a milder flavor and more versatility than regular round cabbage, bok choy is a vegetable to get to know.

## selection and storage

The name bok choy simply means white vegetable and is a catch-all term for many related Asian cabbages. In Hong Kong there are more than 20 varieties! Here the most common is the bok choy with green leaves and thick white stems. Sold in loose heads, it resembles romaine lettuce. You will also find a smaller version, usually labeled baby bok choy. The choy with green stems is often referred to as Shanghai choy. Then there is choy sum with small yellow flowers, and tatsoi with glossy round leaves. Don't let the different names confuse you. All the varieties can almost always be used interchangeably and have similar flavors. Look for firm stalks and crisp green leaves with no wilting. Store bok choy loosely wrapped in the crisper drawer and use it within a few days.

## preparation

Bok choy can be stir-fried, steamed, boiled, deep fried and even enjoyed raw. Remove the stem end to separate the leaves and rinse well. For larger bok choy you may want to separate stems from leaves since stems can take longer to cook. To shred bok choy leaves, stack them and roll them into a tight cylinder, then slice into narrow strips.

## recipe suggestions

Bok choy fits into most stir-fries. Some of the smaller varieties are beautiful and tasty simply steamed and drizzled with sesame oil. Raw, shredded bok choy is a natural for a slaw. Add it to soups at the last minute or use the leaves to wrap rice bundles.

# mongolian vegetables

- 1 package (14 ounces) firm tofu
- 4 tablespoons soy sauce, divided
- 1 tablespoon dark sesame oil
- 1 large head bok choy (about 1½ pounds)
- 2 teaspoons cornstarch
- 1 tablespoon peanut or vegetable oil
- 1 red or yellow bell pepper, cut into short thin strips
- 2 cloves garlic, minced
- 4 green onions, cut into ½-inch pieces
- 2 teaspoons sesame seeds, toasted*

*To toast sesame seeds, spread seeds in small skillet. Shake skillet over medium-low heat 3 minutes or until seeds begin to pop and turn golden.*

## nutrients per serving:

**Calories** 427
**Calories from Fat** 49%
**Protein** 28g
**Carbohydrate** 27g
**Fiber** 8g

**Total Fat** 23g
**Saturated Fat** 2g
**Cholesterol** 0mg
**Sodium** 2,311mg

**1.** Press tofu lightly between paper towels to drain excess water; cut into ¾-inch squares. Place in shallow dish. Combine 2 tablespoons soy sauce and sesame oil in small bowl; drizzle over tofu. Let stand while preparing vegetables.

**2.** Cut stems from bok choy leaves; slice stems into ½-inch pieces. Cut leaves crosswise into ½-inch slices.

**3.** Blend remaining 2 tablespoons soy sauce into cornstarch in small bowl until smooth.

**4.** Heat peanut oil in wok or large skillet over medium-high heat. Add bok choy stems, bell pepper and garlic; stir-fry 5 minutes. Add bok choy leaves and green onions; stir-fry 2 minutes.

**5.** Stir cornstarch mixture and add to wok along with tofu mixture. Stir-fry 30 seconds or until sauce boils and thickens. Sprinkle with sesame seeds.

*Makes 2 main-dish or 4 side-dish servings*

# Broccoli

Broccoli may be an everyday vegetable, but its versatility and nutrition make it an extraordinary food. The dark green head is made of thousands of tiny flower buds. Enjoy broccoli's flower power often.

## benefits

Broccoli is a member of the cabbage or cruciferous family. Like its cousin cabbage, it is high in vitamin A, vitamin C, vitamin K and fiber. In fact, per serving it has cabbage beat for all of these nutrients. If that weren't enough, fresh broccoli is one of the most affordable vegetables and is easily available year round!

## selection and storage

Select broccoli with florets that are dark green, compact and tightly clustered. Yellow flowers

are a sign that it's way past its prime. Check the stem end, too. It should look moist, not dried or cracked. Most broccoli is the standard green variety, but especially at farmers' markets you may see gorgeous purple heads of broccoli or the even more exotic, conical chartreuse heads of romanesco broccoli. Store unwashed broccoli loosely wrapped in your refrigerator's crisper drawer and use it within a few days.

## preparation

Broccoli stems are often discarded, but if you peel the tough outer skin the stem can be sweet and delicious. You will need to cook the stem a few minutes longer than the florets. Stir-frying or steaming broccoli until crisp-tender is the preferred cooking method. Long cooking brings out

broccoli's strong cabbagey aroma and dulls the color. Broccoli is popular raw as part of a crudités offering, but it is more tender and digestible if blanched first. Prepare an ice water bath in a sink or large bowl. Bring water to a boil, add the broccoli florets and cook only for a minute or so. Drain and transfer to the ice water for about 30 seconds to stop the cooking and preserve the color. Drain again and refrigerate until ready to use.

## recipe suggestions

Broccoli's bold flavor pairs well with starches like pasta and rice. A simple sauté in olive oil with garlic, salt, pepper and a pinch of hot red pepper flakes is a quick side dish. To convert even broccoli haters, roast or grill broccoli until it is almost tender and browned in spots.

# Broccoli Rabe

Broccoli rabe (also called rapini or broccoli raab) is broccoli's gutsy Italian cousin and actually more closely related to turnips than broccoli. Use it to add zing to bland foods like pasta or potatoes.

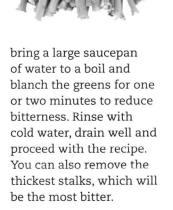

## benefits

Broccoli rabe has a similar nutritional profile to ordinary broccoli, but has more vitamin A and fewer calories. Like broccoli, it's rich in phytonutrients that can protect against cancer. While it may look like a baby version of broccoli, rabe has a bitter edge that pairs well with spicy or starchy ingredients.

## selection and storage

Cool weather brings out the best in broccoli rabe, but it is available year round. Choose bright green leaves and plump, but slender stems. Unlike broccoli, with rabe the stems and leaves are the tasty part of the plant. Avoid bunches that have flowering buds. Younger plants are milder, so choose those with smaller leaves and moist stem ends. A good sniff helps—there should not be a cabbagey smell. Broccoli rabe will last up to four days refrigerated in a plastic bag. Don't wash it until you're ready to cook it.

## preparation

Broccoli rabe can be cooked as you would regular broccoli, but it cooks more quickly so it's even more important to keep a close watch or you'll end up with limp and pungent greens. You can boil, steam, stir-fry, sauté or microwave. Broccoli rabe's bitterness is appreciated in Italy, but American palates aren't as accepting. To enjoy a less assertive broccoli rabe, bring a large saucepan of water to a boil and blanch the greens for one or two minutes to reduce bitterness. Rinse with cold water, drain well and proceed with the recipe. You can also remove the thickest stalks, which will be the most bitter.

## recipe suggestions

It's not surprising that broccoli rabe is a natural in Italian recipes. Try combining it with hearty whole grain pastas like orecchiette, rotini or ziti. A classic preparation is broccoli rabe sautéed in extra virgin olive oil with plenty of garlic and a sprinkling of red pepper flakes to smooth the bitterness. Blanched broccoli rabe is also a healthy and delicious addition to soups.

37

# Brown Rice

Whole grain brown rice would be easy to love even if it weren't so good for you. The mild, slightly nutty flavor and satisfying texture are indispensable in a plant-based diet.

## benefits

All rice starts out brown; to make it white, it must be processed and polished. This removes the bran and a lot of the germ layer as well as most of the nutrients. In fact, more than 65 percent of the B vitamins, 60 percent of the iron and all of the fiber are lost in white rice compared to brown.

## selection and storage

Now that it is a popular health food, it's easy to find short or long grain brown rice and even brown basmati. All brown rice is considerably more perishable than white rice because it still contains the oil-rich germ and fatty acids, which are prone to spoiling. If purchasing brown rice in a package, check for a use-by date. If you're buying in bulk, make sure the bins are covered and that the store has a good turnover to ensure freshness. You can store brown rice for six months in normal conditions; seal it airtight and refrigerate or freeze for longer storage.

## preparation

Cooking brown rice is a lot like cooking white rice, but it takes a little longer. The ratio for long or medium grain brown rice is usually 2¼ cups of water to 1 cup of rice. Rinse the rice in a strainer. Bring the water to a boil in a saucepan and add salt if you wish. Stir in the rice, reduce the heat to low, cover and cook without stirring or lifting the lid for 45 minutes. Short on time? Next time make more rice than you need and freeze the extra in resealable freezer bags. You can defrost it as needed in the microwave. Quick-cooking and instant brown rice are also available and have the same good nutrition.

## recipe suggestions

It's easy to swap white rice for brown in a side dish or a stir-fry. Short grain brown rice is stickier than long grain, so it's a good choice for vegetarian sushi, rice cakes or rice pudding. Try medium or long grain brown rice with beans or chickpeas, as a breakfast cereal or added to soups.

# picante pintos and rice

- 2 cups dried pinto beans, sorted and rinsed
- 1 can (14½ ounces) no-salt-added stewed tomatoes
- 1 cup coarsely chopped onion
- ¾ cup coarsely chopped green bell pepper
- ¼ cup sliced celery
- 4 cloves garlic, minced
- ½ small jalapeño pepper, seeded and chopped
- 2 teaspoons dried oregano
- 2 teaspoons chili powder
- ½ teaspoon ground red pepper
- 2 cups chopped kale
- 3 cups hot cooked brown rice

1. Place beans in large saucepan; add water to cover beans by 2 inches. Bring to a boil over high heat; boil 2 minutes. Remove pan from heat; let stand, covered, 1 hour. Drain beans; discard water. Return beans to saucepan.

2. Add 2 cups water, tomatoes, onion, bell pepper, celery, garlic, jalapeño pepper, oregano, chili powder and ground red pepper to saucepan; bring to a boil over high heat. Reduce heat to low. Simmer, covered, about 1½ hours or until beans are tender, stirring occasionally.

3. Gently stir kale into bean mixture. Simmer until kale is tender. Serve over rice.

*Makes 8 servings*

## nutrients per serving:

| | |
|---|---|
| **Calories** 270 | **Total Fat** 1g |
| **Calories from Fat** 4% | **Saturated Fat** <1g |
| **Protein** 13g | **Cholesterol** 0mg |
| **Carbohydrate** 53g | **Sodium** 35mg |
| **Fiber** 13g | |

# Brussels Sprouts

Brussels sprouts look like cute miniature cabbages and share many of the same nutritional benefits. Whole or shredded, sautéed or steamed, sprouts are versatile and fun to eat.

## benefits

Like their cruciferous cousins, brussels sprouts are full of phytonutrients that help protect against cancer. In addition they are high in vitamin A, vitamin C, potassium and fiber. Many nutritionists recommend eating cruciferous vegetables like cabbage, kale and sprouts several times a week. Brussels sprouts provide the benefits along with a slightly sweet, nutty taste and firm texture. Chances are, if you think you don't like brussels sprouts you've probably only had them overcooked.

## selection and storage

Freshness is crucial to ensuring sweet-tasting sprouts and late fall to early winter is prime season. Brussels sprouts grow clustered around a single stalk several feet long and can sometimes be purchased that way especially at farmers' markets. The heads should be small and firm, not puffy or wilted and should have no loose or yellowing leaves. Refrigerate unwashed sprouts in an airtight plastic bag and use them as soon as possible. While they may not look any different, the flavor of brussels sprouts can become strong and cabbagey in a matter of days.

## preparation

Remove any loose leaves from brussels sprouts, trim the stems, wash and pat dry. If you're cooking them whole, cut a shallow "X" into the stem ends of larger sprouts so that heat can penetrate the sprouts to cook more evenly. Keep a careful watch when boiling or steaming brussels sprouts since you don't want to overcook them, which can happen suddenly. To test doneness, insert a knife into the stem end; it should be barely tender. Brussels sprouts are also delicious oven roasted. For quicker cooking in a skillet, cut brussels sprouts into pieces or shred them.

## recipe suggestions

Don't limit brussels sprouts to the obligatory Thanksgiving side dish. They can be roasted or sautéed along with carrots, potatoes or other vegetables. Brussels sprouts can be shredded and added to slaws. Try adding cooked sprouts to grain dishes, too.

## brussels sprouts in orange sauce

   4 cups fresh brussels sprouts
     Grated peel of 1 orange
   1 cup fresh orange juice
   ½ cup water
   ½ teaspoon cornstarch
   ¼ teaspoon red pepper flakes (optional)
   ¼ teaspoon ground cinnamon
     Salt and black pepper

1. Combine brussels sprouts, orange peel, orange juice, water, cornstarch, red pepper flakes, if desired, and cinnamon in medium saucepan. Simmer, covered, 6 to 7 minutes or until sprouts are nearly tender.

2. Uncover and simmer, stirring occasionally, until most of liquid has evaporated. Season with salt and pepper. *Makes 4 servings*

# Bulgur Wheat

Bulgur wheat has a mild flavor, cooks in minutes and takes well to many different seasonings. This delicious whole grain is a staple of Middle Eastern cookery and is easy to make part of your healthy diet.

## benefits

Bulgur wheat consists of wheat kernels that have been cooked, dried and crushed. Since it is minimally processed, it remains high in protein, fiber and minerals, just like whole wheat. Bulgur wheat is more nutritious than white rice and has more fiber and fewer calories than brown rice. Wheat has been turned into bulgur and appreciated since at least 2800 B.C. It's even mentioned in the Bible!

## selection and storage

You will see bulgur wheat also spelled bulgar, bulghur and burghul. It is sometimes confused with cracked wheat, but bulgur is different since it has been precooked. Bulgur wheat comes in fine, medium or coarse grind. The fine grind is most readily available and perfect for tabbouleh salad, as a breakfast cereal or as a substitute for rice. Medium and coarse grinds can be used in stews, soups, baked goods and for meatless burgers, chilis and tacos. Purchase bulgur from a market with a high turnover. Stored in an airtight container or resealable plastic bag in a cool, dry place, bulgur should last one year.

## preparation

Bulgur wheat just might be the world's healthiest convenience food. Since it is precooked you are only softening the grains. Fine grind bulgur usually calls for one part bulgur to two parts liquid. Simply pour the boiling liquid over the bulgur, stir, cover and wait 7 to 10 minutes or until the liquid is absorbed. Then fluff the grain as you would rice. Check package directions as cooking instructions can vary based on the type and grind of wheat. Cooked bulgur can be stored in an airtight container in the refrigerator for several days.

## recipe suggestions

Just about anywhere you would use rice or couscous, bulgur wheat may be used instead. Add bulgur to soups and salads for extra nutrition. Make a hearty one-dish meal with bulgur, beans or lentils and greens. Create a bulgur pilaf with dried fruit and nuts. And don't forget the tabbouleh!

# far east tabbouleh

- 1½ **cups boiling water**
- ¾ **cup uncooked bulgur wheat**
- 2 **tablespoons lemon juice**
- 2 **tablespoons reduced-sodium teriyaki sauce**
- 1 **tablespoon olive oil**
- ¾ **cup diced seeded cucumber**
- ¾ **cup diced seeded tomato**
- ½ **cup thinly sliced green onions**
- ½ **cup minced fresh cilantro or parsley**
- 1 **tablespoon minced fresh ginger**
- 1 **clove garlic, minced**

1. Combine water and bulgur in medium bowl. Cover with plastic wrap; let stand 10 to 20 minutes or until bulgur is puffed and liquid is absorbed.

2. Combine bulgur, lemon juice, teriyaki sauce and oil in large bowl. Stir in cucumber, tomato, onions, cilantro, ginger and garlic until well blended. Cover; refrigerate 4 hours, stirring occasionally. *Makes 4 servings*

# Butternut Squash

Brighten your fall and winter table with the gorgeous orange flesh and slightly sweet, mellow flavor of butternut squash in soups, stews, risottos and much more.

## benefits

It's probably no surprise that this colorful yellow-orange vegetable is a gold mine of vitamin A. Like other winter squash, it's also rich in fiber. To make it even more appealing, butternut squash can have many personalities depending on how it is prepared. Roasting brings out the inherent sweetness and nuttiness. Puréed, the flesh becomes almost buttery and creamy.

## selection and storage

The first rule of choosing a winter squash is to find one that is rock solid. Press hard to make sure there are no soft spots since that indicates either an immature squash or one that's way past its prime. The stem should be firm and corky. If it's missing, beware—the opening that's left can allow bacteria to enter and spoil the flesh. Butternut squash will keep for months if it's in good shape to begin with and stored in a dry place at cool room temperature. Refrigerate pieces of squash once it is cut open. You can also purchase butternut squash frozen or precut in the refrigerated produce section.

## preparation

The hardest part of preparing a whole butternut squash is cutting it into pieces. Always wash the squash first. Even though you're not eating the skin, bacteria on it can end up inside. Use a large, sharp knife and keep the squash steady on a cutting board. To cut it into cubes or peel it, first cut it in half between the neck and bulb portion. Cut the bulb portion in half and scoop out the edible seeds and stringy pulp. (For a real treat, roast the seeds for a snack.) Peel the skin with a sharp vegetable peeler.

## recipe suggestions

Add cubed butternut squash to soups or stews or serve it as a side dish roasted and tossed with pasta or brown rice. Puréed squash is perfect in a fall soup or as a healthy change from mashed potatoes. Top plain baked butternut squash with brown sugar, nutmeg and cinnamon.

# jamaican black bean stew

- 2 cups uncooked brown rice
- 2 pounds sweet potatoes
- 3 pounds butternut squash
- 1 can (about 14 ounces) vegetable broth
- 1 large onion, coarsely chopped
- 3 cloves garlic, minced
- 1 tablespoon curry powder
- 1½ teaspoons ground allspice
- ½ teaspoon ground red pepper
- ¼ teaspoon salt
- 2 cans (about 15 ounces each) black beans, rinsed and drained
- ½ cup raisins
- 3 tablespoons fresh lime juice
- 1 cup diced tomato
- 1 cup diced peeled cucumber

1. Prepare rice according to package directions. Meanwhile, peel sweet potatoes; cut into ¾-inch chunks to measure 4 cups. Peel squash; remove seeds. Cut into ¾-inch cubes to measure 5 cups.

2. Combine sweet potatoes, squash, broth, onion, garlic, curry powder, allspice, red pepper and salt in Dutch oven. Bring to a boil; reduce heat to low. Cover and simmer 15 minutes or until sweet potatoes and squash are tender. Add beans and raisins; simmer 5 minutes or until heated through. Stir in lime juice.

3. Serve stew over brown rice; top with tomato and cucumber.            *Makes 8 servings*

## nutrients per serving:

**Calories** 463
**Calories from Fat** 7%
**Protein** 16g
**Carbohydrate** 102g
**Fiber** 10g

**Total Fat** 4g
**Saturated Fat** 1g
**Cholesterol** 0mg
**Sodium** 439mg

# Cabbage

A member of the cruciferous vegetable family along with broccoli, cauliflower and kale, cabbage is popular in cuisines around the world. (Think kim chee, colcannon and sauerkraut.)

## benefits

Cabbage provides fiber, vitamin C, potassium and folate. Savoy cabbage and bok choy provide beta-carotene, and bok choy is an important source of calcium.

## selection and storage

There are many types of cabbage, including green, red, napa, savoy and bok choy (see page 34). Green and red cabbage are the most common; both have round heads with tightly packed leaves and a delicate flavor. Select green and red cabbage with tight, compact heads that look crisp and

fresh with few loose leaves. Napa cabbage, also called Chinese cabbage, is a loosely packed elongated head of light green leaves and thick stalks. Savoy cabbage is round with curly, deeply ridges leaves. Store whole heads of cabbage, unwashed, in plastic bags in the refrigerator in the crisper drawer for up to two weeks. One pound of cabbage yields about 4 cups shredded (2 cups cooked).

## preparation

Discard outer leaves if loose or limp. Slice red cabbage with a stainless steel knife (pigment in red cabbage can react with carbon steel and turn the leaves blue) and add lemon juice or vinegar to the cooking liquid to maintain its bright red color. Steam or stir-fry (in a nonaluminum pan) to preserve nutrients until crisp-tender, 10 to 12 minutes for wedges or 5 minutes for shredded.

Cook cabbage only until it is crisp-tender as overcooking results in an unpleasant odor and strong flavor.

## recipe suggestions

Napa cabbage and bok choy work well in stir-fries while savoy cabbage is perfect for stuffing. Try bulgur or quinoa in place of meat in traditional stuffed cabbage recipes. Try kim chee as a condiment with your favorite stir-fry or make a reuben-style sandwich by piling sauerkraut on a grilled vegan burger and serve on rye bread with vegan mayonnaise and ketchup. For a quick, hearty Irish colcannon, sauté sliced onions and cabbage in olive oil in a large skillet until tender. Add cooked red potatoes and slightly mash everything together with salt, pepper and olive oil.

# mu shu vegetables

- 3 tablespoons reduced-sodium soy sauce
- 2 tablespoons dry sherry
- 1½ tablespoons minced fresh ginger
- 2 teaspoons cornstarch
- 3 cloves garlic, minced
- 1½ teaspoons sesame oil
- 1 tablespoon peanut oil
- 3 leeks, slivered
- 3 carrots, peeled and julienned
- 1 cup thinly sliced fresh shiitake mushrooms
- 1 small head napa or savoy cabbage, shredded (about 4 cups)
- 2 cups mung bean sprouts, rinsed and drained
- 8 ounces firm tofu, cut into strips
- 12 (8-inch) fat-free flour tortillas, warmed
- ¾ cup finely chopped peanuts
- ⅔ cup prepared peanut sauce

1. Mix soy sauce, sherry, ginger, cornstarch, garlic and sesame oil in small bowl until smooth; set aside.

2. Heat peanut oil in wok over medium-high heat. Add leeks, carrots and mushrooms; stir-fry 2 minutes. Add cabbage; stir-fry 3 minutes or until tender. Add bean sprouts and tofu; stir-fry 1 minute or until hot. Stir soy sauce mixture; add to wok. Cook and stir 1 minute or until sauce is thickened.

3. Spread each tortilla with about 1 teaspoon peanut sauce. Spoon ½ cup vegetable mixture onto bottom half of each tortilla; sprinkle with 1 tablespoon peanuts. Roll up to enclose filling. Serve with remaining peanut sauce.

*Makes 6 servings*

## nutrients per serving:

**Calories** 477
**Calories from Fat** 32%
**Protein** 19g
**Carbohydrate** 64g

**Fiber** 18g
**Total Fat** 18g
**Saturated Fat** 3g
**Cholesterol** 0mg
**Sodium** 1,043mg

# Capers

These tangy little pickled flower buds add a salty, sour kick to many foods that would otherwise get flavor from cheese.

## benefits

Capers are the perfect condiment to add extra flavor and texture, sprinkled on Italian focaccia, Mediterranean hummus and Greek salad, or stirred into a zesty tomato sauce.

## selection and storage

Capers are the unripened flower buds of the bush Capparis spinosa, a native of the Mediterranean. After the buds are harvested, they are sun-dried and then packed in vinegar, brine or salt. They range in size from the very small French nonpareil to larger Italian and Spanish varieties and stemmed giant caper berries that can be the size of an olive. Capers are sold at large supermarkets and specialty food stores.

Look for them near the jarred olives, pickles and roasted red peppers. Jarred capers packed in brine will last for nine months in the refrigerator while salt-packed capers will last up to six months stored at room temperature.

## preparation

Capers need very little preparation. It's a good idea to rinse capers before using, especially those packed in salt, to remove excess salt and brine. Sprinkle capers over a finished dish or add them at the end of the cooking time.

## recipe suggestions

Use capers in any dish that needs some livening; they work well in tomato sauces, salad dressings and vegetable dishes. They also complement many Mediterranean, Spanish and Italian dishes such as roasted cauliflower, peperonata, sautéed kale or spinach. Try making a zesty vegan pasta puttanesca by replacing the anchovy paste with some extra capers and a splash of brine from the jar. For breakfast, spread some Creamy Cashew Spread (see page 53) on your favorite vegan bagels and top with tomatoes, cucumber, red onion and capers.

# roasted vegetable salad with capers and walnuts

- 1 pound small brussels sprouts, trimmed
- 1 pound unpeeled small Yukon Gold potatoes, cut into halves
- ¼ teaspoon salt
- ¼ teaspoon black pepper
- ¼ teaspoon dried rosemary
- 5 tablespoons olive oil, divided
- 1 red bell pepper, cut into bite-size chunks
- ¼ cup walnuts, coarsely chopped
- 2 tablespoons capers, drained
- 1½ tablespoons white wine vinegar

1. Preheat oven to 400°F.

2. Cut a shallow "X" in bottoms of brussels sprouts; place in roasting pan. Add potatoes; sprinkle with salt, black pepper and rosemary. Drizzle with 3 tablespoons oil; toss to coat. Roast 20 minutes. Stir in bell pepper; roast 15 minutes or until tender. Transfer to large bowl; stir in walnuts and capers.

3. Whisk remaining 2 tablespoons oil and vinegar in small bowl until blended. Pour over salad; toss to coat. Serve at room temperature.

*Makes 6 to 8 servings*

**Potluck Tip:** To bring this salad as a potluck dish, prepare in advance. Cover and refrigerate up to one day. Serve at room temperature.

## nutrients per serving:

| | |
|---|---|
| **Calories** 239 | **Total Fat** 15g |
| **Calories from Fat** 53% | **Saturated Fat** 2g |
| **Protein** 5g | **Cholesterol** 0mg |
| **Carbohydrate** 24g | **Sodium** 208mg |
| **Fiber** 5g | |

# Carrots

Although often dismissed as food for rabbits and dieters, carrots' crunchy sweetness and stellar nutritional profile make them perfect for everyone.

## benefits

Carrots are a super food that provide invaluable health benefits through beta-carotene and insoluble fiber, including protecting eyesight, keeping the skin healthy and shielding the body from infections.

## selection and storage

Carrots are available year round both with their leafy green tops and without. Either way, look for firm, bright orange carrots with smooth skin; medium carrots are tender while thicker carrots may have a larger fibrous core making them tough. Avoid carrots that are limp or black near the top, which indicates that they are not fresh. Immediately remove any leafy green tops and store carrots in a plastic bag in the crisper drawer of the refrigerator for up to two weeks.

## preparation

Thoroughly scrub whole carrots to remove soil contamination. Carrot skin is perfectly edible, but it's a good idea to remove it to get rid of any pesticide residue. Contrary to the popular belief that vegetables are more nutritious in their raw form, the nutrients in lightly steamed carrots are actually more usable by your body than those in raw carrots because cooking breaks down their tough cell walls, releasing beta-carotene. One pound of carrots will yield about 3 cups chopped or sliced, or 2$\frac{1}{2}$ cups shredded.

## recipe suggestions

Carrots are a versatile vegetable, appearing in breakfast (carrot juice), dessert (carrot cake) and everything in between. Besides being a natural for crudités, carrots add color and crunch to salads, stir-fries and sandwiches. They're an essential part of mirepoix, the classic soup base of carrots, celery and onion sautéed in olive oil. And, of course, they're delicious on their own lightly steamed and topped with herbs, sea salt and olive oil, or roasted and glazed with orange juice, brown sugar and freshly ground black pepper. You can even use old carrots left in the refrigerator a little past their expiration date to make a flavorful homemade vegetable stock. Simmer carrots, celery, herbs and unpeeled garlic and onion in a large pot of water about an hour. Remove vegetables with a slotted spoon and season the broth with salt and pepper to taste.

# carrot ginger cupcakes

- 3 cups all-purpose flour
- ⅓ cup coarsely chopped pecans
- 2 teaspoons baking powder
- 1 teaspoon baking soda
- 1 teaspoon salt
- ½ teaspoon ground cinnamon
- ¾ cup water
- 3 tablespoons ground flaxseed
- 1½ cups granulated sugar
- ½ cup vegetable oil
- 1½ cups (3 sticks) dairy-free margarine, divided
- 1 pound carrots, shredded
- Grated peel of 2 oranges
- Juice of 2 oranges, divided
- 2½ tablespoons grated fresh ginger, divided
- 1 tablespoon plus 1 teaspoon vanilla, divided
- 4½ cups powdered sugar

**1.** Preheat oven to 350°F. Line 24 standard (2½-inch) muffin cups with paper baking cups.

**2.** Whisk flour, pecans, baking powder, baking soda, salt and cinnamon in medium bowl. Process water and flaxseed in food processor until well blended.

**3.** Beat granulated sugar, oil and ½ cup margarine in large bowl with electric mixer at medium speed until light and fluffy. Beat in flaxseed mixture. Add carrots, orange peel, ⅓ cup orange juice, 2 tablespoons ginger and 1 tablespoon vanilla; mix well. Add flour mixture; mix just until combined. Spoon batter evenly into prepared muffin cups.

**4.** Bake 22 to 25 minutes or until toothpick inserted into centers comes out clean. Cool in pans 10 minutes. Remove and cool completely.

**5.** Beat remaining 1 cup margarine and 1 teaspoon vanilla in large bowl with electric mixer at medium speed until creamy. Gradually beat in powdered sugar. Beat in remaining ¼ cup orange juice and ½ tablespoon ginger. Beat at medium-high speed at least 1 minute or until fluffy. Frost cupcakes and garnish.

*Makes 24 cupcakes*

# Cashews

Blended to a creamy purée, cashews make a decadent spread, while whole cashews are a tasty snack and the perfect addition to your favorite recipes.

## benefits

Like all nuts, cashews are a good source of protein and healthy unsaturated fat, which is especially important for vegans who might need extra protein in their diet. Cashews also contain beneficial amounts of iron and vitamin E.

## selection and storage

Cashews grow from the base of the cashew apple, an edible but tart apple most often used to make vinegar and liqueur. Cashew nuts are always sold shelled since they are a member of the same family as poison ivy and an oil on their shells can produce an allergic reaction similar to that caused by contact with these toxic plants. Although some cashews are labeled raw, all commercially sold cashew nuts have been treated with heat to destroy any trace residue of the shell oil. Oil-roasted cashews have a rich nutty flavor and are widely available, as are dry-roasted cashews which are lower in fat than oil-roasted cashews. Always store cashews in an airtight container in a cool, dry place. They last two to four weeks at room temperature, up to six months in the refrigerator and one year in the freezer. One ounce of cashews is 15 to 20 nuts, and a pound equals about 3 cups.

## recipe suggestions

Cashews make a fantastic snack on their own, but they can also be used in a variety of dishes. Toss a handful into your favorite stir-fry, salad or pasta dish just before serving, or pour melted dark chocolate over small piles of cashews and let stand until set for a quick salty-sweet treat. Easily make your own cashew butter by processing nuts in a food processor until the consistency of peanut butter is reached (this takes a few minutes). For a creamy sandwich spread and toast topper, try the recipe on the next page. Ground cashews can also be used as a filling for raw vegan cheesecakes.

## nutrients per serving:

**Calories** 136
**Calories from Fat** 66%
**Protein** 4g

**Carbohydrate** 8g
**Fiber** 1g
**Total Fat** 11g

**Saturated Fat** 2g
**Cholesterol** 0mg
**Sodium** 197mg

## creamy cashew spread

- **1 cup raw cashews**
- **2 tablespoons lemon juice**
- **1 tablespoon tahini**
- **½ teaspoon salt**
- **½ teaspoon freshly ground pepper**
- **2 teaspoons minced fresh herbs, such as basil, parsley or oregano (optional)**

**1.** Rinse cashews and place in medium bowl. Cover with water by at least 2 inches. Soak 4 hours or up to overnight.

**2.** Drain cashews, reserving soaking water. Place cashews, lemon juice, tahini, salt, pepper and 2 tablespoons soaking water in food processor. Process 4 to 6 minutes or until smooth. Add additional water if needed to achieve desired texture.

**3.** Refrigerate until ready to serve. Stir in herbs just before serving. Use as spread or dip for hors d'oeuvres, as a sandwich spread or pasta topping. Thin with additional liquid as needed.

*Makes about ½ cup (6 servings)*

# Cauliflower

If cauliflower brings to mind a mushy, slightly smelly veggie on your dinner plate when you were a child, it's time to give it another try! With the right preparation it can become a favorite part of your vegan diet.

## benefits

Yes, this cruciferous vegetable kind of looks like a brain, which serves as a reminder of how good cauliflower is for your entire body. After citrus fruits, cauliflower is your next best natural source of vitamin C, an antioxidant vitamin with wide-ranging benefits including defending blood vessels from damage and lowering the risk of high blood pressure. Cauliflower is popular in Middle Eastern, Mediterranean and especially Indian cuisines, where it can be found fried and slow-simmered in stews, paired with potatoes for a rich, satisfying curry and stuffed in samosas.

## selection and storage

White cauliflower is most common but purple cauliflower is also available. (You may even encounter something called "broccoflower," a cross between broccoli and cauliflower that looks like light green cauliflower.) Though cauliflower is available year round, its peak season is from late fall to early spring. Look for firm, creamy white heads with compact florets; avoid cauliflower with speckling or brown spots, or leaves that have signs of yellowing. Store cauliflower unwashed in a perforated plastic bag up to one week. Cooked cauliflower does not store well.

## preparation

Remove the outer leaves and trim the stem end. Break off the florets and wash them under running water. A medium head of cauliflower weighs about two pounds; one pound of trimmed cauliflower yields about $1^1/_2$ cups of florets. Steam or microwave cauliflower until crisp-tender (be sure not to overcook it), and then dress it with olive oil, salt, pepper and herbs.

## recipe suggestions

Try substituting cauliflower for broccoli in your favorite recipes, or serve it raw with any dip. For the best flavor, try roasting it. Slice through the head and core, making cross-section slices. Spread the slices on an oiled baking sheet, drizzle with olive oil, sprinkle with salt and pepper and bake at 450°F about 25 minutes until golden and tender, turning once.

# Chickpeas

Also called garbanzo beans and ceci (CHEE-chee) beans, chickpeas are delicious, nutritious and extremely versatile in the vegan diet.

## benefits

Like other legumes, chickpeas are packed with protein, iron and fiber, making them especially important for vegans. They are vital parts of Mediterranean, Middle Eastern and Indian cuisines, and are featured in such fare as hummus, falafel, minestrone soup and chana masala. (Indian food is know for being vegetarian-friendly but be aware that many dishes contain ghee, a type of clarified butter with a high smoke point.)

## selection and storage

Canned chickpeas are widely available and retain their flavor and shape

better than most other varieties of canned beans, but you'll get better taste and texture by using dried chickpeas. One pound of dried beans (2½ cups) will yield about 6 cups of cooked beans. Store dried chickpeas in an airtight container in a cool, dry place for up to a year.

## preparation

To cook dried chickpeas, place them in a large pot and add water to cover by 2 inches. Soak for 8 to 12 hours, then change the water and cook over medium heat at a gentle simmer 30 to 45 minutes or until tender. To quick soak chickpeas, place them in the pan in which they will be cooked. Cover with water by 3 inches. Bring to a boil and boil for 2 minutes. Remove from the heat; cover and let stand for one hour, then proceed with recipe or cook until tender. Cooking dried beans uncovered will result in a firmer texture.

## recipe suggestions

Chickpeas make a great addition to soups, stews, salads and grain dishes. They pair especially well with greens like kale, broccoli rabe and Swiss chard. Simmer soaked dried chickpeas until almost tender and then add greens; simmer until everything is tender. Season with olive oil, garlic salt and pepper (add curry powder and red pepper flakes for extra flavor) and serve over couscous or small pasta like orecchiette. For a quick homemade hummus, drain 1 can (20 ounces) of chickpeas and place in a food processor. Add ¼ cup tahini, the juice of half a lemon, a garlic clove, salt and a dash of ground red pepper, if desired. Process one to two minutes or until smooth and fluffy.

# Chipotle Peppers

Dark, smoky and zesty, chipotle peppers add piquant flavor and depth to your favorite Mexican-inspired dishes.

## benefits

Chipotle peppers are dried smoked jalapeño peppers. In fact, chipotle is the Nahuatl word for "smoked chile pepper." To make chipotles, growers leave jalapeños on the plant until late in the season when they turn bright red, then harvest them and smoke them for several days until they are dried. Chipotles rank medium-low on the Scoville scale, a measurement of the capsaicin in chile peppers, indicating their level of heat. (For comparison, bell peppers are unranked because they have no measurable capsaicin while habaneros rank medium-hot.) Chipotles add just a touch of heat and a delightful smoky richness to many dishes.

## selection and storage

Chipotle peppers are most often available canned in adobo sauce, a dark red sauce made of ground chiles, tomatoes, herbs and vinegar. They are also available dried. Store dried peppers in an airtight container in a cool, dry place up to one year. Unopened canned peppers will last two or more years. Once open, store leftover peppers and adobo sauce in an airtight container in the refrigerator for about a month or freeze for up to four months.

## preparation

Canned chipotles are ready to use but dried chipotles should be softened unless you plan on grinding them into a powder. To reconstitute dried chipotles, soak them in hot water until they're soft and then slice, chop or mince. You can also add a dried chile directly to soups, stews or pots of beans for a subtle smoky flavor. Remove it before serving, or remove and discard the stem, chop the pepper and return it to your stew. When using canned chipotles, try stirring some of the adobo sauce into your dish for extra flavor.

## recipe suggestions

Try chipotles in Mexican and Tex-Mex dishes like chilis, rice and beans, pozole and black bean soup. Purée chipotles with some adobo sauce and use as a marinade for tofu or seitan or as a sauce for vegan tacos or fajitas. The smoky flavor of chipotles also complements baked beans, veggie burgers and tomato sauce for pasta or pizza. You can also mince or purée chipotles and add them to condiments such as barbecue sauce, ketchup, vegan mayonnaise and salsa.

# Coconut Milk

Coconut milk makes a rich, delicious vegan substitute for milk products in cooking and in beverages.

## benefits

Coconut milk is a coconut product made by simmering shredded coconut in water and then straining out and squeezing the coconut to extract the liquid. It adds body and creamy richness to Thai and tropical cuisines.

## selection and storage

Look for unsweetened coconut milk in cans in the Asian section of the supermarket. There is a wide range of coconut products beyond coconut milk, but don't be confused—they cannot be used interchangeably.

Coconut water is the liquid from the inside of a coconut and is sold for drinking, not cooking. Coconut milk beverages act as a milk substitute. Coconut cream is similar to coconut milk, but is thicker because it contains less water. Often a layer of coconut cream will separate from the milk in a can of regular coconut milk. Shake cans well before opening, or whisk milk and cream together in a bowl. Cream of coconut is sweetened coconut cream and is used primarily in desserts and drinks like piña coladas.

## preparation

Coconut milk is an essential ingredient in Thai red, green and panang curries. Be aware that most Thai food contains fish sauce (nam pla), so it's safer to make Thai food yourself with vegetarian fish sauce rather than taking your chances with take-out. If you can't find vegetarian fish sauce, you can make your own or substitute mushroom soy sauce to add rich umami flavor. Try cooking basmati or jasmine rice in a mixture of half coconut milk and half water. Coconut milk also works well in rice puddings, smoothies and hot chocolate.

## recipe suggestions

Try making a quick vegan ice cream: Combine 2 cans unsweetened coconut milk and 1/2 cup sugar in medium saucepan. Cook over medium-low heat, whisking constantly, until smooth. Refrigerate until cold. Process in an ice cream maker according to manufacturer's directions. Add a chopped candy bar, chocolate chips or fresh fruit during the last few minutes of stirring, if you like. Transfer to a freezer storage container and freeze until firm.

# Couscous

Couscous is a versatile staple in the vegan pantry. Not only is it the perfect accompaniment to hearty legume and vegetable stews, it also makes a great side dish, breakfast and even dessert.

## benefits

Couscous, which is made from semolina flour like pasta, is a staple of North African cuisine, particularly in Algeria, Morocco, Tunisia and Libya where it generally accompanies a root vegetable stew or meat stew. In Tunisia, it is flavored with harissa, a hot and spicy sauce made with chiles, garlic, cumin and olive oil. Couscous is traditionally cooked in the top of a couscoussière, a pot specially designed to cook couscous in the fragrant steam from a stew cooking below it. Couscous is slightly more nutritious than rice and pasta, containing more vitamins and minerals than pasta, such as riboflavin, niacin, vitamin $B_6$ and folate, and more protein than rice.

## selection and storage

Couscous is available plain and as mixes with seasoning packets. Virtually all couscous has been presteamed and dried, which cuts preparation time to a matter of minutes. Israeli couscous (ptitim) is quite different; it is more closely related to orzo. Invented in Israel as a wheat-based substitute for rice during the 1950s when rice was scarce, cooked Israeli couscous resembles a round chewy orzo and makes a fun substitute for small pasta or rice in soups, sides and salads.

## preparation

Bring $1^1/_2$ cups water to a boil in a small saucepan. Stir in 1 cup couscous and remove from heat. Cover and let stand 5 minutes. Fluff with a fork before serving. Add olive oil, salt and saffron threads or turmeric for color and flavor before stirring in the couscous, or do like the Tunisians and stir in a spoonful of harissa.

## recipe suggestions

Serve lentil and bean stews over couscous for a hearty main dish (see the next page). Stir in curry powder, dried cranberries, chopped green onions and toasted almonds for a salad. For breakfast or dessert, stir in cinnamon, raisins, walnuts and a little agave, and top with a splash of soymilk.

# lentil stew over couscous

- 3 cups dried brown lentils (1 pound), sorted and rinsed
- 3 cups water
- 1 can (about 14 ounces) vegetable broth
- 1 can (about 14 ounces) diced tomatoes
- 1 large onion, chopped
- 1 green bell pepper, chopped
- 4 stalks celery, chopped
- 1 medium carrot, sliced
- 2 cloves garlic, chopped
- 1 teaspoon dried marjoram
- ¼ teaspoon black pepper
- 1 tablespoon olive oil
- 1 tablespoon cider vinegar
- 4½ to 5 cups hot cooked couscous

**Slow Cooker Directions**

1. Combine lentils, water, broth, tomatoes, onion, bell pepper, celery, carrot, garlic, marjoram and black pepper in slow cooker. Cover and cook on LOW 8 to 9 hours.

2. Stir in oil and vinegar. Serve over couscous.

*Makes 12 servings*

**Tip:** Lentil stew keeps well in the refrigerator for up to 1 week. Stew can also be frozen in an airtight container for up to three months.

## nutrients per serving:

| | |
|---|---|
| **Calories** 203 | **Total Fat** 2g |
| **Calories from Fat** 9% | **Saturated Fat** <1g |
| **Protein** 11g | **Cholesterol** 0mg |
| **Carbohydrate** 37g | **Sodium** 128mg |
| **Fiber** 4g | |

# Cranberries

Cranberries are a holiday staple, but their tart and tangy flavor make them a favorite year round. They liven up salads and baked goods and make a delicious accompaniment to so much more than your vegan turkey substitute.

## benefits

Cranberries contain phytonutrients that have an antibacterial effect on the body that can prevent or treat certain infections, gum disease and stomach ulcers. They also contain significant amounts of antioxidants and vitamin C.

## selection and storage

Cranberries are grown in bogs on low vines in the cooler climates of northern Europe and the U.S. (Massachusetts, Wisconsin and Washington) and are harvested September through October, just in time for the holidays. Fresh cranberries are available late September through December in the produce section of the

supermarket. They are packed in 12-ounce plastic bags, which yield 3 cups whole berries (2$^1/_2$ cups chopped berries). Store fresh cranberries tightly wrapped in the refrigerator for one to two months or freeze for up to one year. Frozen cranberries can be found year round, but it's a good idea to buy a few extra bags when they're fresh and freeze them yourself. Canned cranberry sauce, both jellied and whole-berry, is available year round, as are dried sweetened cranberries. Store dried sweetened cranberries in a tightly sealed container or bag in a cool, dry place or the refrigerator up to one year.

## preparation

Rinse fresh or frozen cranberries under cold water and pick out and discard any soft or blemished berries. Frozen cranberries do not need to be thawed before using. To make quick work of chopping whole berries, pulse in a food processor until coarsely or finely chopped.

## recipe suggestions

Transform cranberry sauce into a chutney or compote to garnish potato pancakes, vegetable quesadillas and sandwiches. Blend fresh cranberries, oil and vinegar until smooth for a tangy cranberry vinaigrette. Chopped fresh or frozen cranberries make a great addition to quick breads, muffins, pies, crisps and pancakes. Use dried cranberries just like raisins and add them to your favorite baked goods. They also make a nice addition to salads, couscous, quinoa, oatmeal, cold cereal and trail mix.

# cranberry coconut bars

- **2 cups fresh or frozen cranberries**
- **1 cup dried sweetened cranberries**
- **⅔ cup granulated sugar**
- **¼ cup water**
- **Grated peel of 1 lemon**
- **1¼ cups all-purpose flour**
- **¾ cup old-fashioned oats**
- **½ teaspoon baking soda**
- **½ teaspoon salt**
- **1 cup packed light brown sugar**
- **¾ cup (1½ sticks) dairy-free margarine, softened**
- **1 cup shredded sweetened coconut**
- **1 cup chopped pecans, toasted\***

*\*To toast pecans, spread in single layer on baking sheet. Bake in preheated 350°F oven 5 to 7 minutes or until golden brown, stirring frequently.*

## nutrients per serving:

**Calories** 221
**Calories from Fat** 43%
**Protein** 2g
**Carbohydrate** 29g
**Fiber** 1g

**Total Fat** 10g
**Saturated Fat** 4g
**Cholesterol** 0mg
**Sodium** 148mg

1. Preheat oven to 400°F. Grease and flour 13×9-inch baking pan.

2. Combine fresh cranberries, dried cranberries, granulated sugar, water and lemon peel in medium saucepan. Cook over medium-high heat 10 to 15 minutes or until cranberries begin to pop, stirring frequently. Mash cranberries with back of spoon. Let stand 10 minutes.

3. Combine flour, oats, baking soda and salt in medium bowl. Beat brown sugar and margarine in large bowl with electric mixer at medium speed until creamy. Add flour mixture; beat just until blended. Stir in coconut and pecans. Reserve 1½ cups; press remaining crumb mixture into bottom of prepared pan. Bake 10 minutes.

4. Gently spread cranberry filling evenly over crust. Sprinkle with reserved crumb mixture. Bake 18 to 20 minutes or until center is set and top is golden brown. Cool completely in pan on wire rack. Cut into bars.

*Makes 2 dozen bars*

# Cremini & Portobello Mushrooms

No survey of vegan foods would be complete without the ubiquitous portobello mushroom. Nutritious, hearty and chewy, mushrooms make a perfectly natural meat substitute.

## benefits

Cremini mushrooms are in the same family as the common cultivated white mushroom but have a brown color, firmer texture and richer flavor. Portobello mushrooms are large mature cremini mushrooms that have dried out slightly, which concentrates their flavor and gives them their distinct meaty texture. Mushrooms provide important nutrients including B vitamins, selenium and potassium and are the only plant source of vitamin D.

## selection and storage

Cremini mushrooms are also known as baby portobellos, baby bellas or brown mushrooms, and portobello mushrooms are sometimes labeled with one of their spelling variants: portabello or portabella. Both kinds are available year round in the produce section of the supermarket. Choose mushrooms that are firm and evenly colored with tightly closed caps. Avoid ones that are slimy or have any soft dark spots. Packaged mushrooms can be refrigerated as is, but loose mushrooms should be refrigerated in a paper bag or ventilated container (not in the crisper drawer) for up to a week. One pound of mushrooms will yield about 6 cups of slices or 2 cups of cooked mushrooms.

## preparation

To clean mushrooms, wipe with a damp paper towel or rinse briefly and dry thoroughly. Do not soak mushrooms because they will become mushy. Trim cremini mushroom stems or remove, if desired. Portobellos' dark gills are perfectly edible but are sometimes removed so they don't darken other ingredients. Do remove and discard the tough stems, however, unless the recipe directs otherwise. Add mushrooms to stir-fries, casseroles, pasta dishes and beans and greens.

## recipe suggestions

Grilled portobellos are a nice change of pace from frozen vegan patties. Remove the stems and marinate the caps in vinaigrette for 15 minutes. Grill over medium-high heat 5 minutes per side or until tender and serve on buns with condiments, or slice and add to a salad. Grill some eggplant, bell peppers and onions at the same time for a roasted vegetable panini. For an appetizer, try stuffing cremini mushrooms with bread crumbs, spinach and roasted red pepper and baking until hot (stuff portobellos with the same mixture for an entrée).

# mushroom gratin

- 4 tablespoons dairy-free margarine, divided
- 1 small onion, minced
- 8 ounces (about 2½ cups) sliced cremini mushrooms
- 2 cloves garlic, minced
- 4 cups cooked elbow macaroni, rotini or other pasta
- 2 tablespoons all-purpose flour
- 1 cup plain soymilk
- ½ teaspoon salt
- ½ teaspoon black pepper
- ½ teaspoon dry mustard
- ½ cup fresh bread crumbs
- 1 tablespoon extra virgin olive oil

**1.** Preheat oven to 350°F. Melt 2 tablespoons margarine in large skillet over medium-high heat. Add onion; cook and stir 2 minutes. Add garlic and mushrooms; cook and stir 6 to 8 minutes or until vegetables soften. Stir in pasta; set aside.

**2.** Melt remaining 2 tablespoons margarine in medium saucepan over low heat. Whisk in flour; cook and stir 2 minutes without browning. Stir in soymilk. Bring to a boil over medium-high heat whisking constantly. Reduce heat to maintain a simmer. Add salt, pepper and mustard. Whisk 5 to 7 minutes or until sauce thickens. Add sauce to pasta mixture; stir gently to combine.

**3.** Spoon mixture into shallow baking dish or casserole. Top with bread crumbs and drizzle with olive oil. Cover; bake 15 minutes. Uncover and bake 10 minutes or until bubbly and browned. *Makes 8 servings*

# Cucumbers

Cool and refreshing, cucumbers make a fresh addition to salads, sandwiches, cold soups and crudités.

## benefits

One of the oldest known cultivated vegetables, cucumbers are readily available year round and can easily be grown in home gardens. At more than 95 percent water with a mild flavor, they make a perfect light snack and can be added to just about anything.

## selection and storage

There are two basic types of cucumbers—those eaten fresh (slicing cucumbers) and those used for pickling. The most common slicing cucumbers are the field variety, about six to nine inches long with dark green skin and tapered ends. Hothouse cucumbers, also called English cucumbers, are longer (one to two feet) and thinner with smooth skin and almost no seeds. Small kirby cucumbers are used for making pickles, and are sometimes available at the supermarket or farmers' markets. Cucumbers are available year round but are best from May through July. Store whole cucumbers in the vegetable drawer for up to one week. Tightly wrap cut cucumbers in plastic wrap and store in the refrigerator for two to three days. One 7-inch cucumber yields 2 cups sliced or chopped.

## preparation

Wash cucumbers thoroughly just before using. Supermarket cucumbers are covered with an edible wax to protect them from moisture loss and to improve shelf life. If you prefer not to eat the wax you can peel the cucumber or use a produce rinse to help remove it. Cucumber seeds are edible, but they can be removed by cutting the cucumber in half lengthwise and scooping out the seeds with a spoon.

## recipe suggestions

Indian raita, Greek tzatziki and Turkish cacik are all versions of the cool and refreshing Mediterranean cucumber yogurt salad that pairs well with your favorite hot and spicy stews and curries. Combine thick plain dairy-free yogurt, chopped garlic and mint or other fresh herbs and chopped or shredded cucumbers. Or try an Asian cucumber salad made with shredded cucumber, thinly sliced red onion, rice vinegar, a splash of mirin and toasted sesame seeds for garnish.

# greek salad with dairy-free "feta"

### Dairy-Free "Feta"

- 1 package (14 ounces) firm or extra-firm tofu
- ½ cup extra virgin olive oil
- ¼ cup lemon juice
- 2 teaspoons salt
- 2 teaspoons Greek or Italian seasoning
- ½ teaspoon black pepper
- 1 teaspoon onion powder
- ½ teaspoon garlic powder

### Salad

- 1 pint grape tomatoes, halved
- 2 seedless cucumbers, sliced
- 1 yellow bell pepper, cut into slivers
- 1 small red onion, cut in thin slices

1. Cut tofu horizontally into 2 pieces. Place on cutting board lined with paper towels; top with layer of paper towels. Place weighted baking dish on top of tofu. Let stand 30 minutes to drain. Pat tofu dry and crumble into large bowl.

2. Combine oil, lemon juice, salt, Greek seasoning and black pepper in small jar with lid; shake to combine well. Reserve ¼ cup of mixture for salad dressing. Add onion powder and garlic powder to remaining mixture. Pour over tofu and toss gently. Refrigerate overnight or at least 2 hours.

3. Combine tomatoes, cucumbers, bell pepper and onion in serving bowl. Add tofu "feta" and reserved dressing. Toss gently.

*Makes 4 to 6 servings*

## nutrients per serving:

**Calories** 399
**Calories from Fat** 72%
**Protein** 12g
**Carbohydrate** 17g
**Fiber** 4g
**Total Fat** 32g
**Saturated Fat** 4g

**Cholesterol** 0mg
**Sodium** 1,397mg

# Curry Paste

Fragrant, delicious homemade curries are made fast and foolproof with premade curry pastes.

## benefits

Bottled curry pastes are great for vegans who love Thai and Southeast Asian dishes but have trouble finding a restaurant that makes them without fish sauce or shrimp paste. All you need for a superb homemade curry is a spoonful of curry paste, a can of coconut milk (see page 57) and some cut-up vegetables and tofu.

## selection and storage

The word curry means "sauce" and is used to describe both spice blends and the dishes made with them. The dried curry powder called for in Indian dishes is a mixture of as many as 20 different spices including chiles, cinnamon, cumin, fennel seed, ginger, coriander and turmeric. Southeast Asian curry paste is a blend of fresh ingredients like lemongrass,

galangal, Thai basil, fresh chiles, onion, garlic, kaffir lime peel and oil. Red and green curry pastes are the most commonly available in supermarkets; they are essentially the same except red curry is made from fresh red chiles and green curry is made from green chiles. Yellow curry is also very similar, except that it is often made from yellow chiles and contains turmeric, which makes it yellow. Less commonly available are masaman curry paste, made with dried spices that give it a more Indian flavor, and panang curry paste, a mild Malaysian curry paste that often contains peanuts. Curry pastes are available in jars and pouches in the Asian section of large supermarkets. Be sure to read ingredient lists carefully because some chile pastes may contain

ghee (clarified butter), fish sauce or shrimp paste. Refrigerate jars of curry paste after opening.

## recipe suggestions

Make a Thai curry by heating chile paste, coconut milk and vegetable broth to a simmer in a wok or large saucepan. Add tofu and cut-up vegetables, simmer until tender and serve over rice noodles or jasmine rice. Curry paste also makes a zesty addition to stir-fries, soups and marinades for vegetables, tofu and seitan.

# Dairy-Free Margarine

Just because you're vegan doesn't mean you can't enjoy rich and delicious homemade baked goods. Dairy-free margarine delivers the same texture and buttery crumb in your favorite cookies and cakes without the butter.

## benefits

Margarine was invented (by a Frenchman!) in 1869 to imitate the texture and taste of butter without milk. Since margarine is made from vegetable oil it is free of animal fat and cholesterol. In fact, the entire vegan diet is basically cholesterol-free because cholesterol is not found in measurable quantities in plants. Dairy-free margarine offers vegans the same buttery consistency for baked goods and functions the same as a spread for toast and a topping for vegetables without the animal fat.

## selection and storage

Dairy-free margarine comes in two forms: as sticks like butter and in tubs. Use the stick form as a one-to-one substitute for butter in baking recipes. Some tub margarine is acceptable for baking (check the package) but in general it is best left as a topping for toast and as a substitute for butter in cooking. There is often more water or air added to tub margarine to create its always-spreadable consistency so it will not measure the same as stick margarine or butter. A word of caution: many margarines on the market are labelled nondairy, but nondairy does not mean dairy-free or vegan. Products labeled nondairy can still contain whey and casein, so check the label for the word "milk", which by law must be present on products containing any milk product, no matter how obscure the name. Also check for the Kosher designation "pareve" (or "parve"), which means that the product is dairy-free. Dairy-free margarine can be hard to find in regular supermarkets, although most large stores should have at least one product. Natural and health food stores are your best bet for the widest selection of products.

## recipe suggestions

Dairy-free margarine makes a good roux and a decent béchamel with unflavored soymilk. Whisk equal amounts of margarine and flour in a saucepan over low heat until blended and smooth, then add enough soymilk until the desired consistency is reached. Serve over pasta and vegetables for a rich and creamy entrée. Replace the soymilk with vegetable broth for a velouté (a gravy-like sauce) to serve over mashed potatoes and other vegetables.

# Dairy-Free Milk

Doing without dairy has never been easier. Choose soymilk, rice milk, almond milk, even hemp milk. These tasty dairy replacements can do pretty much everything milk can do.

## benefits

When choosing a dairy-free milk, check the nutritional label. Most dairy-free milks are fortified with calcium and vitamin $B_{12}$ to bring them nutritionally closer to cow's milk. There are many variations and even the same kind of milk will have different numbers depending on whether it's sweetened and/or fortified. Soymilk is the highest in protein with almost as much as dairy milk. Rice milk has a thinner consistency than soymilk and less protein. Almond milk is lower in calories and sugar than most other dairy milks. Hemp milk is high in omega-3 and omega-6 fatty acids. Choose the milk that has the flavor and nutritional profile that's right for you.

## selection and storage

Most dairy-free milks are available in aseptically sealed shelf-stable cartons in the health food aisle as well as in the refrigerated dairy case. While dairy-free milks can all be substituted for each other, the different flavors and textures may influence how you use them. Rice milk is slightly sweet, so it works well in dessert recipes, but is not as appropriate in savory dishes. Soymilk is a good substitute in baking since it is similar to cow's milk in protein content and texture. Almond milk is rich and nutty, but has a flavor profile that can clash with savory dishes. For drinking or pouring on cereal, choose whichever you like best. Aseptic cartons can usually be stored for several months. Check use-by dates and remember that once opened, cartons should be refrigerated and used within the suggested time limit.

## preparation

Dairy-free milks are made by cooking beans or nuts with water, puréeing, straining and adding sweeteners or vitamins. You can make some dairy-free milks in a blender at home. Check the internet for recipes.

## recipe suggestions

Dairy-free milk can replace cow's milk one-to-one in most recipes. To create a replacement for buttermilk, stir 1 tablespoon of lemon juice or vinegar into 1 cup of dairy-free milk and let it sit for 5 minutes to sour. For cream sauces use a dairy-free creamer for better consistency.

# breakfast rice pudding

- 2 cups vanilla soymilk, divided
- ¾ cup uncooked brown rice
- ⅓ cup packed light brown sugar
- ½ teaspoon ground cinnamon
- ½ teaspoon salt
- ¼ cup golden raisins or dried sweetened cranberries (optional)
- ½ teaspoon vanilla
- Mixed berries (optional)

1. Bring 1½ cups soymilk to a boil in medium saucepan. Stir in rice, brown sugar, cinnamon and salt. Return to a boil. Reduce heat; cover and simmer 15 minutes.

2. Stir in remaining ½ cup soymilk and raisins, if desired. Cover and simmer 10 to 15 minutes or until rice is tender. Remove from heat; stir in vanilla. Serve with berries, if desired.

*Makes 4 servings*

**Note:** Rice thickens as it cools. For a thinner consistency, stir in additional soymilk just before serving.

## nutrients per serving:

**Calories** 136
**Calories from Fat** 66%
**Protein** 4g
**Carbohydrate** 8g
**Fiber** 1g
**Total Fat** 11g
**Saturated Fat** 2g
**Cholesterol** 0mg
**Sodium** 197mg

# Dairy-Free Sour Cream & Yogurt

Dairy-free sour cream and yogurt offer similar taste and texture as their regular counterparts, and can be used in your favorite recipes. Some dairy-free yogurt even comes complete with helpful probiotics.

## benefits

A little tangy sour cream or yogurt goes a long way to make vegetable dips and fruit smoothies more satisfying, and a dollop on spicy stews can help cool the fire. A few years ago, vegan options for sour cream and yogurt alternatives were quite limited. Fortunately, as the vegan diet has become more mainstream and much media attention has been focused on milk and gluten sensitivities (together and separately), more dairy-free "dairy" products have become available. Vegan substitutes for milk, cheese, ice cream, sour cream and yogurt are widely available in health and natural food stores and a more limited selection is available in regular supermarkets.

## selection and storage

Soy- and tofu-based sour cream substitutes are fairly easy to find and have the same sour, tangy taste and creamy texture of regular. Cultured soy yogurt is the most common vegan yogurt alternative and works well as a substitute for regular in recipes. Coconut milk yogurt can be found in both regular and thicker Greek-style varieties, both flavored and unflavored, and also works well in recipes. It does have a mild coconut flavor, so make sure it complements your recipe. Rice milk yogurt is best left to eating plain as it is thinner than other alternatives and doesn't substitute well for regular yogurt in recipes. Less common but also available is fruit-based arrowroot-thickened yogurt, which is free of all allergens, and nut-milk yogurt. Many dairy-free yogurts are fortified with probiotics ("good" bacteria) and vitamins.

## recipe suggestions

Use dairy-free sour cream as a topping for your favorite spicy Mexican foods and chilis. Substitute one-to-one for regular sour cream in dip recipes and serve as a topping for loaded baked potatoes along with salsa, chopped green onions and avocado slices. Check the package first, but some vegan sour creams can be substituted for regular in baked goods like coffee cake, cheesecake and muffins. Use dairy-free yogurt to make creamy fruit smoothies, parfaits, cool and refreshing cucumber-yogurt salad (see page 64) and fruit dips.

# chilled cucumber soup

1 large cucumber, peeled and coarsely
   chopped
¾ cup dairy-free sour cream or silken tofu
¼ cup packed fresh dill
½ teaspoon salt
⅛ teaspoon ground white pepper
1½ cups vegetable broth
   Dill sprigs

**1.** Place cucumber in food processor; process until finely chopped. Add dairy-free sour cream, ¼ cup dill, salt and pepper; process until fairly smooth.

**2.** Transfer mixture to large bowl; stir in broth. Cover and chill at least 2 hours or up to 24 hours. Ladle into shallow bowls; garnish with dill sprigs.          *Makes 4 (¾-cup) servings*

# Dates

These wrinkly, dry little fruits pack a nutritional punch and a satisfying amount of sweetness while being versatile enough to include in any meal throughout the day.

## benefits

Dates should be a pantry staple for all vegans with a sweet tooth. These little nuggets of nature's candy can satisfy a craving without the bother of deciphering the mysterious language of candy bar and sweet snack food wrappers to determine if the treat is vegan and has any nutritional value. Dates are loaded with both soluble and insoluble fiber, potassium and iron.

## selection and storage

Dates are the fruit of the date palm tree, a native of the deserts of North Africa and the Middle East that can also be found in parts of California and Arizona. Dates have long been a staple of the Middle Eastern diet, especially

for travelers as dates have a low moisture content and keep well long after they are picked. There are many varieties of dates in varying degrees of size, sweetness and moistness. Large, soft Medjool dates are available in the fall and are ideal for snacking or stuffing. Deglet Noor dates, the most common variety in the United States, are available year round in the produce section of large supermarkets. Packaged dates are available pitted, unpitted or chopped. Dates will keep for up to a year well wrapped in the refrigerator.

## preparation

To make slicing and chopping dates easier, chill them first. The colder they are, the easier they are to slice. Date purée, a simple blend of dates that have been soaked in hot water, can be substituted for some of the sugar in baked goods to add richness, moistness and fiber. It can also be

used as a filling for bar cookies, as in the recipe on the next page.

## recipe suggestions

Add chopped dates to granola, oatmeal and quick breads like classic date-nut bread. Try making a sweet side dish by adding chopped dates, dried cranberries, almonds, cinnamon, nutmeg and a little curry powder to cooked couscous or quinoa. Dates often get paired with salty foods like bacon and cheese for appetizers. For a vegan sweet and salty combo, stuff dates with peanut butter, toasted pecans or walnuts and sprinkle with coarse salt.

# whole wheat date bars

- 4½ **cups chopped dates**
- 2½ **cups water**
- 2¾ **cups whole wheat flour**
- 2 **cups old-fashioned oats**
- ¼ **cup all-purpose flour**
- ¼ **cup packed brown sugar**
- 1½ **teaspoons salt**
- ½ **teaspoon ground cinnamon**
- ½ **cup maple syrup**
- ½ **cup (1 stick) cold margarine, cut into small pieces**
- 1 **cup vegetable shortening, at room temperature**

**1.** Preheat oven to 400°F. Spray 13×9-inch baking dish with nonstick cooking spray.

**2.** Cook and stir dates and water in large saucepan over medium heat 10 minutes or until thickened. Remove from heat.

**3.** Combine whole wheat flour, oats, all-purpose flour, sugar, salt and cinnamon in large bowl. Stir in maple syrup. Cut margarine into flour mixture with pastry blender or two knives until coarse crumbs form. Mix in shortening until dough holds together. Place 5 cups dough in prepared baking dish. Press firmly onto bottom and partially up sides of dish to form crust. Pour date mixture evenly into crust. Top with remaining dough.

**4.** Bake 25 minutes or until golden brown. Cool slightly before cutting into bars.

*Makes 2 dozen bars*

# Dried Mushrooms

Go beyond basic mushrooms with exotic dried wild mushrooms. Chanterelles, porcinis and morels bring a subtle, earthy taste to any dish.

## benefits

Mushrooms are an excellent way to make vegetable dishes more savory and flavorful; they enhance the flavor of other ingredients without overwhelming them. Mushrooms are high in umami, Japanese for "pleasant savory taste" and the fifth basic taste along with sweet, bitter, salty and sour. Ripe tomatoes and spinach are also high in umami; other sources include non-vegan foods like cheeses and cured meats.

## selection and storage

Unlike cultivated white and brown mushrooms, wild mushrooms are not consistently available fresh. Instead, they are dried and packaged individually or in a mixed assortment. The most commonly available dried mushrooms are shiitakes and oyster mushrooms. Less common are chanterelles, porcini and wood ear mushrooms. You may also find the elusive morel dried. It has a woodsy, smoky, deep and complex flavor. Dried mushrooms are available in supermarkets, usually in the produce section, and online. They may seem expensive but keep in mind that fresh mushrooms are 90 percent water; dried mushrooms soak up water like a sponge and are quickly restored to their fresh size and weight. Also, dried mushrooms are very flavorful so you don't need to use a lot. Store dried mushrooms in an airtight container in a cool, dry place for up to one year; refrigerate or freeze for longer storage.

## preparation

To reconstitute dried mushrooms, soak them in warm water for 20 to 30 minutes or until softened, or in boiling water for 15 to 20 minutes. Strain the soaking liquid through a fine strainer or coffee filter to catch dirt particles if you plan on using it. (Try it in soups, stews and pasta sauces or to cook risotto and polenta.) Rinse mushrooms to remove any embedded dirt and drain on paper towels.

## recipe suggestions

Mushrooms make great soup, or a nice addition to any vegetable soup or stew. They are also a perfect topping for polenta or crostini. Sauté chopped reconstituted mushrooms in olive oil with some fresh thyme, salt and pepper for ten minutes, adding some red wine halfway through cooking. For an Italian classic, cook Arborio rice in vegetable broth mixed with soaking liquid and add chopped porcinis at the end. Garnish with arugula and toasted pine nuts.

# buddha's delight

- 1 package (1 ounce) dried shiitake mushrooms
- 1 package (14 ounces) firm tofu, drained
- 1 tablespoon peanut or vegetable oil
- 2 cups bite-size asparagus pieces
- 1 medium onion, cut into thin wedges
- 2 cloves garlic, minced
- ½ cup vegetable broth
- 3 tablespoons hoisin sauce
- ¼ cup coarsely chopped fresh cilantro or thinly sliced green onions

**1.** Place mushrooms in small bowl; cover with warm water. Soak 20 minutes to soften. Drain over fine strainer, squeezing out excess water into measuring cup; reserve. Discard mushroom stems; slice caps.

**2.** Place tofu on cutting board lined with paper towels; cover with more paper towels and top with weighted baking dish. Press for 15 minutes. Cut tofu into ¾-inch cubes or triangles.

**3.** Heat oil in wok or large skillet over medium-high heat. Add asparagus, onion wedges and garlic; stir-fry 4 minutes.

**4.** Add mushrooms, ¼ cup reserved mushroom liquid, broth and hoisin sauce. Reduce heat to medium-low. Simmer, uncovered, 3 minutes or until asparagus is crisp-tender.

**5.** Stir in tofu; heat through, stirring occasionally. Sprinkle with cilantro.

*Makes 2 main-dish or 4 side-dish servings*

## nutrients per serving:

**Calories** 332
**Calories from Fat** 38%
**Protein** 20g
**Carbohydrate** 36g
**Fiber** 8g
**Total Fat** 15g
**Saturated Fat** 3g

**Cholesterol** <1mg
**Sodium** 553mg

# Edamame

Edamame is the Japanese name for fresh green soybeans. This high-protein legume is delicious both straight from the pod as a snack and shelled and tossed into your favorite stews, salads and stir-fries.

## benefits

Unlike most plant sources of protein, edamame is a complete protein, which means that it contains all of the essential amino acids (building blocks of protein) that your body can't produce and must get from food. It is also low in calories and a rich source of fiber.

## selection and storage

Edamame are grown on bushes (the name means "beans on branches") and harvested at the peak of ripeness. Edamame is rarely found fresh but is widely available frozen, both shelled and in the pod. Store fresh edamame in the refrigerator for up to two weeks; frozen edamame will last up to six months.

## preparation

To cook edamame shelled or in the pod, boil, steam, sauté or microwave until the beans are tender but firm; check the package for cooking times and be sure not to overcook. In Japan, the beans are boiled in salted water and then squeezed out of the pods with the teeth (the tough pods are discarded). They are often served this way at Asian restaurants in the United States as an appetizer often sprinkled with coarse salt or with soy sauce for dipping.

## recipe suggestions

Add shelled edamame to stir-fries, curries, salads, casseroles and pasta dishes; add it anywhere you would normally add green peas or beans. For a healthy salty snack, combine 10 ounces of shelled edamame, 2 teaspoons vegetable oil and ¼ teaspoon wasabi powder in a large bowl. Spread on a baking sheet and bake at 375°F for 12 to 15 minutes or until golden brown, stirring once. Remove to a large bowl and sprinkle with kosher salt.

# spring vegetable ragoût

- 1 tablespoon olive oil
- 2 leeks, thinly sliced
- 3 cloves garlic, minced
- 1 package (10 ounces) frozen corn
- ½ pound yellow squash, sliced
- 6 ounces frozen shelled edamame
- 1 bag (4 ounces) shredded carrots
- 1 cup vegetable broth
- 3 cups small cherry tomatoes, halved
- 1 teaspoon dried tarragon
- 1 teaspoon dried basil
- 1 teaspoon dried oregano
  Salt and black pepper (optional)
  Minced fresh parsley (optional)

1. Heat oil in large skillet over medium heat. Add leeks and garlic; cook and stir just until fragrant. Add corn, squash, edamame, carrots and broth; cook and stir until squash is tender.

2. Stir in tomatoes, tarragon, basil and oregano. Reduce heat to low. Cover and simmer 2 minutes or until tomatoes are soft. Season with salt and pepper, if desired. Garnish with parsley.           *Makes 6 servings*

## nutrients per serving:

| | |
|---|---|
| **Calories** 156 | **Total Fat** 5g |
| **Calories from Fat** 26% | **Saturated Fat** <1g |
| **Protein** 7g | **Cholesterol** 0mg |
| **Carbohydrate** 25g | **Sodium** 111mg |
| **Fiber** 5g | |

# Eggplant

This versatile meat-replacing vegetable is part of many popular ethnic dishes including Indian curries, Italian caponata, Middle Eastern baba ghanoush and French ratatouille.

## benefits

If it seems odd to call something so bulbous and purple "eggplant", take a look at the small white variety. (Outside of North America, the eggplant is called aubergine.) Like the tomato and avocado, this member of the nightshade family is actually a fruit, specifically a berry, but treated like a vegetable. Eggplant is a hearty low-calorie plant substitute for meat in stews, soups and stir-fries.

## selection and storage

The most common eggplant found in supermarkets is large and oblong, weighing about one pound, with shiny dark purple skin. Japanese eggplant is slender, about five inches long, with purple or striped white skin and a sweeter and milder flavor. Italian eggplant looks like a miniature version of regular purple eggplant with more delicate skin and flesh. White eggplant is small and egg shaped with tough skin that requires peeling and firm, sweet flesh. Chinese eggplant varies in size and shape: it can be long, slender and lavender, or round, tiny and white. For the best flavor, choose small eggplant with thinner skin as larger ones tend to be seedy, tough and bitter. Eggplant becomes bitter with age so purchase it within a few days of using. Store it unwashed in a cool, dry place for a day or two, or in a plastic bag in the refrigerator for up to five days.

## preparation

Eggplant skin is perfectly edible, but older eggplants with thicker skin and white eggplants should be peeled with a vegetable peeler. To help reduce any bitterness, slice or halve the eggplant, season both sides with salt and let stand 30 minutes. Drain and blot dry before cooking. Eggplant can be baked, roasted, grilled, steamed or sautéed. It is notorious for soaking up oil like a sponge so if you're going to fry it, make sure is has a nice thick coating of breading to prevent too much oil absorption.

## recipe suggestions

Substitute dairy-free cheese alternative for the cheese in classic eggplant parmigiana, or sprinkle the top with toasted chopped almonds or walnuts before serving. Eggplant makes a nice addition to vegetable lasagna and pasta dishes, and is also delicious stuffed with other vegetables and grains.

## szechuan eggplant

- 1 pound Asian eggplants
- 2 tablespoons peanut or vegetable oil
- 2 cloves garlic, minced
- ¼ teaspoon red pepper flakes *or*
-      ½ teaspoon hot chili oil
- ¼ cup vegetable broth
- ¼ cup hoisin sauce
- 3 green onions, cut into 1-inch pieces
-    Toasted sesame seeds* (optional)

*To toast sesame seeds, spread in small skillet. Shake skillet over medium-low heat 3 minutes or until seeds begin to pop and turn golden.*

1. Cut eggplants into ½-inch strips.

2. Heat oil in wok or large nonstick skillet over medium-high heat. Add eggplant, garlic and red pepper flakes; stir-fry 7 minutes or until eggplant is very tender and browned.

3. Reduce heat to medium. Add broth, hoisin sauce and green onions to wok; cook and stir 2 minutes. Sprinkle with sesame seeds.

*Makes 4 to 6 servings*

# Egg Replacers

Be warned: eggs are everywhere. It's not all bad news, though. There are many ways to replace eggs in your home cooking and baking that give good results.

## benefits

Packaged and prepared foods that seem like they should be vegan (no meat or cheese) may contain eggs. Commercially made baked goods, pancakes, waffles, donuts, crackers and pretzels usually contain eggs, as do many pastas, noodles and meat substitute products, so check packages carefully for words like "ovo", "albumin" and "globulin." Keep in mind that many sauces and entrées at restaurants contain eggs, as does most food that's battered and fried (eggs help the coating stick). Fortunately there are many different ways to replace eggs, and in most cases your results will be the same.

## selection and preparation

For replacing eggs in baked goods, the easiest and most consistent replacement is powdered egg replacer. Simply mix the powder with water following package directions and add it to your recipe. In many baked goods requiring no more than three eggs, like cookies and cupcakes, silken tofu is an acceptable egg replacement; use 1/4 cup of tofu to replace each egg. One mashed banana or 1/4 cup of applesauce can fill in for eggs in muffins or quick breads that are sweet or fruity. Ground flaxseed is another acceptable egg substitute that does not impart any noticeable flavor. Combine 1 tablespoon ground flaxseed and 1/4 cup water for each egg and process until well blended in a small food processor or blender. Use right away so that the mixture does not begin to separate. To replace eggs when breading and frying vegetables or tofu, try mixing cornstarch with soymilk or rice milk (see page 127 for an example).

## recipe suggestions

If breakfast doesn't seem the same without eggs, try scrambled tofu instead for a protein-packed egg substitute. Follow the recipe on page 117, or scramble the tofu with some vegan pesto (see page 25) and serve over steamed vegetables. Tofu also makes a nice substitute for eggs in eggless egg salad. Drain and press firm or silken tofu and crumble it into a bowl. Add vegan mayonnaise, salt, pepper and chopped celery, red onion and dill pickle.

## apple & raisin softies

1¾ cups all-purpose flour
½ cup whole wheat flour
1½ teaspoons pumpkin pie spice
½ teaspoon baking soda
½ teaspoon baking powder
½ teaspoon salt
¾ cup (1½ sticks) dairy-free margarine, softened
1 cup packed brown sugar
   Prepared egg replacer equal to 1 egg
½ cup unsweetened applesauce
1 small apple, peeled, cored and finely chopped
1 cup walnuts, chopped
¾ cup raisins

1. Preheat oven to 375°F. Line cookie sheets with parchment paper. Combine all-purpose flour, whole wheat flour, pumpkin pie spice, baking soda, baking powder and salt in medium bowl.

2. Beat margarine and brown sugar in large bowl with electric mixer at medium speed until blended. Add egg replacer, beating until blended. Stir in applesauce. Gradually add flour mixture; beat until well blended. Stir in apple, walnuts and raisins.

3. Drop dough by tablespoonfuls about 2 inches apart onto prepared cookie sheets. Gently flatten with back of spoon.

4. Bake 14 to 16 minutes or until golden brown. Cool cookies on cookie sheets 5 minutes. Remove to wire racks; cool completely.

*Makes 3 dozen cookies*

### nutrients per serving:

**Calories** 120

**Calories from Fat** 43%
**Protein** 2g
**Carbohydrate** 16g
**Fiber** 1g

**Total Fat** 6g
**Saturated Fat** 2g
**Cholesterol** 0mg
**Sodium** 100mg

# Farro

This ancient grain is making a comeback among chefs and foodies. With its chewy texture and nutty flavor, it's easy to see why.

## benefits

Farro (pronounced "FAR-oh") is an ancient grain that is part of the wheat family. It comes from the Mediterranean region, and is possibly one of the first plants to be domesticated in the Middle East. It was a staple food for the Roman legions and kept the masses fed for centuries, but because it's difficult to grow and doesn't have a high yield, it was eventually abandoned in favor of other grains. It was rediscovered in recent culinary history and given a second life as a fancy gourmet grain; it has turned up on the fanciest tables at the best restaurants. Farro makes a nice substitute for rice, pasta and barley in many dishes.

## selection and storage

Farro is often confused with spelt and emmer, possibly because Italians used the word farro to refer to multiple wheatlike kinds of grains. Farro is an oval grain similar in shape to barley, with a firm, chewy texture and nutty taste. It is still grown in parts of Tuscany and is also produced in Washington state. Pearled and whole grain versions are available; whole grain farro is more nutritious but takes longer to cook. Both domestic farro and Italian imports are available at specialty and gourmet food stores and some large supermarkets. Some farro is ground into flour to make bread and pasta, and Italian-made farro pasta is also available.

## preparation

Cook farro like you would most any other grain by simmering it in water or broth until tender. Whole grain farro will cook in about an hour; pearled farro takes half the time. Spelt and barley can be substituted for farro in many recipes but they have different textures and cooking times.

## recipe suggestions

Swap farro for rice or barley in soups and stews. Mix it with vegetables and nuts and use it to stuff bell peppers, eggplant or acorn squash. You can even use it in place of Arborio rice in risotto recipes. It will not result in the same creaminess, but it will have a similar chewy texture and nutty flavor and does not need to be watched and stirred.

# farro veggie burgers

1½ cups water
½ cup pearled farro
2 medium potatoes, peeled and quartered
2 to 4 tablespoons canola oil, divided
¾ cup finely chopped green onions
1 cup grated carrots
2 teaspoons grated ginger
2 tablespoons ground almonds
¼ to ¾ teaspoon salt
½ teaspoon black pepper
½ cup panko bread crumbs
8 whole wheat hamburger buns

## nutrients per serving:

**Calories** 287
**Calories from Fat** 22%
**Protein** 6g
**Carbohydrate** 48g
**Fiber** 6g
**Total Fat** 8g
**Saturated Fat** 1g
**Cholesterol** 0mg
**Sodium** 243mg

**1.** Combine 1½ cups water and farro in medium saucepan. Bring to a boil. Reduce heat and partially cover; cook 25 to 30 minutes or until farro is tender. Drain and cool.

**2.** Meanwhile, place potatoes in large saucepan; cover with water. Bring to a boil; reduce heat and simmer 20 minutes or until tender. Cool and mash potatoes; set aside.

**3.** Heat 1 tablespoon oil in medium skillet over medium-high heat. Add green onions; cook 1 minute. Add carrots and ginger. Cover and cook 2 to 3 minutes or until carrots are tender. Transfer to large bowl; cool completely.

**4.** Combine mashed potatoes and farro with carrot mixture. Add almonds, salt and pepper. Mix well. Shape mixture into 6 patties. Spread panko on plate; coat patties with panko.

**5.** Heat 1 tablespoon oil in large nonstick skillet over medium heat. Cook patties about 4 minutes per side or until golden brown, turning once and adding additional oil as needed. Serve on buns with desired condiments.

*Makes 6 servings*

# Fennel

If you're not familiar with this crunchy Italian vegetable, try it! Sub it for celery in salads and stir it into soups. Don't let the anise flavor deter you; when it's cooked, fennel's flavor mellows and softens.

## benefits

Fennel is rich in folate, fiber, vitamin C and phytonutrients. It is an essential part of Italian and French cuisine, although it is perhaps best known for the fennel seeds that give Italian sausage that particular anise taste and smell. In fact, fennel is sometimes called sweet anise, although the licoricelike flavor of fresh fennel becomes much less aggressive when cooked.

## selection and storage

There are two main types of fennel. Common fennel, a bulbless plant, is the source of fennel seeds, while Florence fennel (finocchio) has a large bulb and is used as a vegetable. The bulbous base is white to pale green with several slender stalks topped with feathery green leaves. Fennel is in season in the fall, winter and early spring but it is available year round in large supermarkets and Italian grocery stores. Select bulbs that are firm, clean and unblemished with fresh feathery tops. Store fennel in the refrigerator in a plastic bag. The bulb will keep for one week; the green tops for two to three days. Store fennel seeds in a cool, dark place for six months.

## preparation

Although the bulb, stalks and leaves are all edible, the bulb is typically the only part that is eaten; the stalks can be tough and the feathery leaves have little flavor, although they make a lovely garnish. Wash the bulb under cold water and trim off the stalks. Trim the bottom of the bulb, leaving 1/8 inch of the base, and remove any dry or discolored outer layers. Cut the bulb into quarters for braising; thinly slice or finely chop for salads or soups. One large bulb of fennel (about one pound) yields about 2 1/2 cups of slices.

## recipe suggestions

Next time you're grilling or roasting vegetables, add some fennel wedges to the mix. You can also boil it with potatoes and garlic and mash everything together for a tasty twist on mashed potatoes. Add it to vegetable stew or classic Italian minestrone, or cut paper-thin slices and add raw to salads.

# Figs

Fresh or dried, figs have a luscious sweetness and succulent, chewy texture that make them unique. No wonder they have been revered for centuries as a sacred fruit.

## benefits

Centuries ago figs were believed to be an aphrodisiac. While that's never been confirmed, we do know that dried figs have one of the highest overall mineral contents of any common fruit. All figs offer a healthy helping of fiber, too, which can aid digestion. They are also a rich source of potassium, which is essential for controlling blood pressure. Figs' flavor is so concentrated that a small amount can add a touch of sweetness to anything from cookies to savory sauces.

## selection and storage

Fresh figs are extremely perishable and are only in season from late June to early fall. They do not ripen after picking and are quite fragile. The most common varieties are the black mission and yellowish Calmyrna. Choose those that have a sweet fragrance and feel tender to a gentle touch. Refrigerate fresh figs, but eat them as soon as possible. Dried figs are available year round and can be stored in the original package at room temperature for at least a month. Once opened, transfer the fruit to a closed container and refrigerate for up to six months.

## preparation

Let fresh figs come to room temperature for the best flavor. Snip off the very tip of the stem and rinse gently. There's no need to peel. Dried figs have a concentrated flavor and dense texture. You'll need to snip off the tough little stem on the top. To soften figs that have become too dry, soak or steam them in water or wine. To chop dried figs, rinse your knife in hot water occasionally to combat stickiness.

## recipe suggestions

Fresh, ripe figs need little embellishment. Dried figs can be poached in wine or water with the addition of cinnamon, ginger and orange peel. A fruit compote made with figs, apples, cranberries and other fall fruits can be dessert by itself or a topping for cereal, pudding or cake. Add chopped figs to breads, cookies and trail mixes.

# Flaxseed

These ordinary looking seeds are tiny, but they are packed with giant nutritional benefits. The omega-3 fatty acids found in flaxseed make it a popular health food.

## benefits

For vegetarians and vegans, getting enough omega-3 fatty acids is a challenge since they are found primarily in cold water fish. Flaxseed is rich in alpha linolenic acid, the plant version of omega-3 fat. In fact, flaxseed is probably the best source of this important nutrient. If you still need convincing, consider the facts that flaxseed is rich in both kinds of beneficial fiber and can be used as an oil or egg substitute.

## selection and storage

Flaxseed can be purchased whole or ground. Color ranges from deep gold to reddish brown, depending on variety, but nutritional benefits are very similar. Since ground flaxseed is extremely perishable, it's best to buy it whole and grind it as needed. While whole flaxseed and ground contain the same nutrients, they are more easily absorbed from ground seed. Purchase flaxseed from someplace with a good turnover and store in an airtight container away from heat, light and moisture, where it will keep fresh for several months. Ground flaxseed should be purchased in a vacuum-sealed package or under refrigeration. Once ground, store the flaxseed meal in the freezer and use it within a few weeks. Discard any flaxseed that tastes at all bitter.

## preparation

You can purchase a special grinder for flaxseed, but a coffee grinder will also work. (Just don't use the same grinder for coffee beans and flaxseed!) It takes only seconds to turn seeds into meal. Some powerful blenders will also grind flax. Make sure you grind a big enough quantity. Very small amounts can just fly around. You can also grind in a mortar and pestle and exercise your arm muscles.

## recipe suggestions

Start the day right. Add ground flaxseed to hot or cold cereal, a smoothie or soy yogurt with fruit. Toast the flaxseed first for an extra nutty flavor. To use flaxseed as an egg replacer, combine 1 tablespoon of ground flaxseed with $1/4$ cup of water for each egg. Blend in a food processor or blender until thick.

# Garlic

Garlic has been credited with everything from increasing strength to scaring away vampires. Its flavor can be subtle or sweet, pungent or spicy, depending on how it is prepared.

## benefits

Research suggests that garlic can help lower high blood pressure and slow hardening of the arteries. It also seems to protect against some sorts of cancers. Garlic is good for you, but it's also a good way to add a whole range of flavors to your vegan kitchen—from the mellow sweetness of roasted cloves to the hot spiciness of raw garlic.

## selection and storage

The most common variety of fresh garlic bulb is covered in a papery white skin. Pink-skinned Italian garlic is sweeter and milder,

but more perishable. Choose garlic bulbs that are firm and plump and store them in a cool dry place away from sunlight. If you have too much fresh garlic to use within a few months, peel it and freeze the cloves. They will become soft, but retain most of their flavor. Do NOT store raw garlic cloves in oil at room temperature as this can cause contamination with botulism. Commercially jarred garlic in oil is safe since it contains preservatives. At the farmers' market you can often purchase young or green garlic, which looks more like green onions and has a delicious mild flavor.

## preparation

To peel garlic cloves, rest them on a cutting board and press down with the broad edge of a knife. The skin will separate and be easy to remove. If there is a green shoot inside a clove, discard it since it can taste bitter. The smaller you cut or press a garlic clove, the stronger its flavor. For a mild touch of garlic flavor add a whole peeled crushed clove to the dish while cooking and remove it before serving. To experience the suave, buttery side of garlic, roast an entire head until tender, then squeeze out the cloves.

## recipe suggestions

Just about any vegetable tastes better with garlic. Add it to the oil when sautéing, stir-frying or roasting. Raw garlic contributes a spicy note to guacamole, hummus and other dips. A crushed garlic clove adds a mild zing to salad dressings. About the only place it doesn't belong is dessert!

# Ginger

Whether fresh, ground or candied, ginger adds irresistible zing to almost any dish from salad to dessert. No wonder it's a favorite spice around the world from South Asian curries to British gingerbread.

### benefits

In ancient China and India ginger was considered a tonic for digestion and a medicine for swollen joints. Ginger was an important trade item for 5,000 years and was so valuable in the 14th century it was worth as much as a whole live sheep! Today ginger's real ability to help with stomach upset and nausea are supported by research. It is also rich in antioxidants that can have anti-inflammatory effects that may help arthritis, so it appears ginger is living up to some of the claims of long ago.

### selection and storage

Fresh ginger is the rhizome (an underground stem) of the ginger plant. It's a knobby, bumpy beige root that you will find in the produce section. Ginger root should be firm and fragrant and free of wrinkling or soft spots. It can be stored at room temperature for up to three weeks. For longer storage, freeze fresh ginger in a sealed bag and thaw slightly to slice off a portion for use. Ground ginger comes from the same plant, but has a different flavor. Candied or crystallized ginger is made from slices of the fresh root that have been cooked in a sugar syrup until sweet and tender. You can make your own or purchase it already prepared.

### preparation

Ginger root has a thin beige skin, which can be rubbed off with a spoon (try a serrated grapefruit spoon) or a paring knife. Grate the dense fibrous root on the small holes of a grater or use a porcelain ginger grater, which can be purchased at an Asian food store. Grating frozen ginger is actually easier. Large quantities of ginger can be grated in a food processor.

### recipe suggestions

Fresh ginger and garlic are the beginnings of almost any stir-fry or curry. Ground ginger is the leading spice in gingerbread and gingersnaps and pairs well with other warm spices like cinnamon and nutmeg. Candied ginger can be enjoyed as is or used in baked goods.

# triple ginger cookies

2 cups all-purpose flour
2 teaspoons baking soda
1 teaspoon ground ginger
½ teaspoon salt
¾ cup (1½ sticks) dairy-free margarine
1¼ cups sugar, divided
¼ cup molasses
Prepared egg replacer equal to 1 egg
1 tablespoon finely minced fresh ginger
1 tablespoon finely minced crystallized
ginger*

*Semisoft sugar-coated ginger slices are preferable to the small dry ginger cubes found on supermarket spice shelves. The softer, larger slices are available at natural foods or specialty stores. If using the small dry cubes of ginger, steep the cubes in boiling hot water a few minutes to soften, then drain, pat dry and mince.

## nutrients per serving:

**Calories** 67
**Calories from Fat** 51%
**Protein** 1g
**Carbohydrate** 8g
**Fiber** 0g
**Total Fat** 4g
**Saturated Fat** 2g
**Cholesterol** 0mg
**Sodium** 143mg

1. Sift flour, baking soda, ground ginger and salt into medium bowl.

2. Melt margarine in small heavy saucepan over low heat; pour into large bowl and cool slightly. Add 1 cup sugar, molasses and egg replacer; mix well. Add flour mixture; mix well. Add fresh ginger and crystallized ginger; mix just until blended. Cover; refrigerate 1 hour.

3. Preheat oven to 375°F. Line cookie sheets with parchment paper or lightly grease. Roll dough into 1-inch balls. Roll in remaining ¼ cup sugar. Place 3 inches apart on prepared cookie sheets. (If dough is very sticky, drop by teaspoonfuls into sugar to coat.)

4. For chewy cookies, bake 7 minutes or until edges just start to brown. For crisper cookies, bake 2 to 4 minutes longer. Cool on cookie sheets 1 minute. Remove to wire racks; cool completely. *Makes 3 dozen cookies*

**Variation:** Roll dough in plastic wrap to form a log. Refrigerate up to one week or freeze up to two months. To bake, bring the dough nearly to room temperature and slice. Dip the tops in sugar and bake as directed in step 4.

# Jalapeño Peppers

Nothing packs more flavor punch than a hot pepper. Jalapeños are the perfect pepper pick. These meaty beauties can vary from a little tingle to red-hot fire depending on the pepper and the preparation.

## benefits

Capsaicin, the chemical that makes chile peppers hot, has been shown to kill cancer cells, relieve nerve pain and help with sinus infections. Jalapeños are also rich in vitamin A and vitamin C. If you've ever had a hot pepper make your nose run, you know that they can help clear your sinuses. It's interesting that hot peppers feature in many cuisines from hot climates—Mexico, Indian, Southeast Asia. The reason may be that they cause us to sweat, which is nature's way of cooling us down.

## selection and storage

There are hundreds of varieties of chile peppers. Jalapeños are favorites since they are readily available, have an herbal, fruity flavor and moderate heat. Anaheim peppers (California green chiles) are larger and quite a bit milder. Serranos are slender, smaller and very hot. Habanero chiles are tiny, orange and much too hot to handle for most folks. Purchase fresh peppers that are smooth and brightly colored. Mature jalapeños are bright red. Most chile peppers can be stored in the crisper drawer of your refrigerator for about one week. You can also freeze jalapeños whole or chopped. They will keep for up to a year.

## preparation

Jalapeños and other hot peppers can sting and irritate your skin and your eyes. The safest way to work with them is to wear latex or rubber gloves. Many recipes suggest removing the seeds and ribs to somewhat mellow the heat. Cut the pepper vertically in half and scoop them out with a small sharp knife. Wash your hands well after handling chiles and be careful not to touch your eyes. The hotness can persist on your hands even after washing. It's a good idea to take a tiny taste of a jalapeño before using it to judge how hot it is.

## recipe suggestions

Jalapeños are integral to Mexican cuisine. Add them to homemade salsa made with any fruit—pineapple and mango are particularly good. They can also add zing to salads and slaws of all kinds.

# gazpacho

3 pounds ripe tomatoes (6 large), divided
1½ cups tomato juice
1 clove garlic
2 tablespoons fresh lime juice
2 tablespoons olive oil
1 tablespoon white wine vinegar
1 teaspoon sugar
½ to 1 teaspoon salt
½ teaspoon dried oregano
6 green onions, sliced
¼ cup finely chopped celery
¼ cup finely chopped seeded cucumber
1 or 2 jalapeño peppers, seeded and minced
2 cups croutons (optional)
1 cup diced avocado
1 red or green bell pepper, chopped
2 tablespoons chopped fresh cilantro

1. Seed and finely chop 1 tomato; set aside.

2. Coarsely chop remaining 5 tomatoes; place in food processor. Add tomato juice and garlic; process until smooth. Press through sieve into large bowl; discard seeds.

3. Whisk lime juice, oil, vinegar, sugar, salt and oregano into tomato mixture. Stir in finely chopped tomato, green onions, celery, cucumber and jalapeños. Cover; refrigerate at least 4 hours or up to 24 hours to develop flavors.

4. Stir soup; ladle into chilled bowls. Top with croutons, if desired, avocado, bell pepper and cilantro. *Makes 4 servings*

## nutrients per serving:

**Calories** 206
**Calories from Fat** 53%
**Protein** 5g
**Carbohydrate** 22g

**Fiber** 7g
**Total Fat** 13g
**Saturated Fat** 2g
**Cholesterol** 0mg
**Sodium** 557mg

# Kale

Kale is a member of the nutritious cabbage family, but with a milder flavor and pretty, frilly green leaves. Try kale simmered, sautéed, added to soups, pastas, gratins and more.

## benefits

Kale is an excellent source of vitamins A and C. It's also one of the best plant sources of readily absorbed calcium, which is especially important for vegans. Winter dishes can become dull and starchy and kale can add interest, nutrition and variety. Kale is at its best in the coldest months and becomes even sweeter after a light frost. Kale even changes its texture to suit the dish. Long simmering makes it sweet and tender, quick stir-frying leaves it chewy and baking makes it crisp and light.

## selection and storage

There are several varieties of kale. Dark green curly kale is the most common. Russian kale has magenta stems and flatter leaves sometimes tinged with red. Tuscan, or dinosaur, kale has flat, dark blue-green leaves with a bumpy surface. All kale should have firm leaves and stems with no yellowing or wilting. Store it, unwashed, in the crisper drawer of your refrigerator in a plastic bag. Use it within four or five days. The flavor becomes stronger and somewhat bitter with long storage.

## preparation

The most time-consuming task when cooking kale is washing it. Dirt and sand can easily hide deep in its leaves. Break off any tough stems and swish kale around in plenty of water. Remove thick stems or ribs by folding leaves in half and pulling the leaf away from the stem. These thick parts take longer to cook than the delicate leaves. Like spinach, kale shrinks a great deal once cooked. One pound of raw kale will yield about 1/2 cup of cooked.

## recipe suggestions

Add kale to any pasta, potato, grain or bean dish where it will contribute color as well as nutrition. Young, tender leaves are delicious raw in salads. Kale can be substituted for spinach, chard or cabbage in most recipes. Even kids like kale chips. Tear kale leaves into one-inch pieces, toss with a little olive oil and seasoned salt and bake until crisp, about 10 minutes.

# Kidney Beans

Kidney beans hide a creamy beige interior under their rusty red or pretty pink skins and have a satisfying, earthy flavor that calls for strong seasonings. What would chili be without them?

## benefits

Vegans know beans count! They provide protein, fiber, B vitamins and amino acids to plant-based diets. Kidney beans also provide iron, an essential nutrient that is hard to get from vegetable sources. Served with rice, kidney beans provide complete protein, including all the essential amino acids that must be obtained from food. Plus, kidney beans are economical, keep for a long time and are available canned or dried.

## selection and storage

Dried kidney beans come in many shades of pink and red. Purchase them

from a market with high turnover. Latin American markets usually have a good selection and reasonable prices. Even dried beans have a shelf life of only about one year and old beans or those that are stored in heat or humidity will never cook properly. Canned beans are an excellent option as well. They retain most of the same nutrients, though they generally have a higher sodium content. Cooked beans will keep tightly covered in the refrigerator up to one week or in the freezer for several months.

## preparation

Cooking dried kidney beans does take time, but it's mostly hands-off. Soaking before cooking not only decreases cooking time, it also eliminates most of the chemicals that can cause intestinal gas, provided you discard the soaking water. Rinse and sort through

the kidney beans first and discard any broken ones or foreign matter. Cover with cold fresh water by at least three inches and discard any beans that float. Soak for at least four hours or overnight. Rinse, drain and cover with fresh water in a large saucepan or Dutch oven. Bring to a boil, skim any foam, reduce heat to a simmer and cover. Kidney beans will take 1 to $1\frac{1}{2}$ hours to cook.

## recipe suggestions

Besides chilis and soups, kidney beans are great in salads since they retain their shape well. Try mixing kidney beans with rice, quinoa or millet to add color and texture. Kidney beans can also be mashed for use in dips or bean burgers.

# Leeks

Their size can fool you. Leeks look like overgrown green onions but cooked, they mellow and soften, providing subtle sweetness and a complex flavor that's a lovely surprise.

## benefits

Leeks have been beloved for centuries and are still used much more frequently in Europe than they are here. As a member of the Allium family, like onion and garlic, leeks share many of the same nutritional benefits. They are a good source of fiber, folic acid and vitamins $B_6$ and C. Since they are milder they make a less forceful presence when substituted for onion and may also be easier to digest.

## selection and storage

Leeks are usually sold tied in bunches of three or four. Smaller leeks with a paler green color are more tender, which is important if you will be cooking them whole. Large leeks with bulbous root ends can be woody and tough. The leaves should be crisp and green with no yellowing. The roots should be attached and pliable, not stiff or dried. Store leeks in the refrigerator crisper drawer well wrapped for up to a week. They are considerably more perishable than onions. Leeks are in season from late fall to spring.

## preparation

Cleaning leeks thoroughly is critical. Dirt and even mud can hide in between the many layers wrapped tightly in concentric circles. Trim off the root and the dark green leaves from the top. You can save the leaves for soup or stock. So that the leek stays together, slit it lengthwise, but stop about an inch from the base. Wash it by holding open the layers and swishing away the grime in plenty of water. If you are using sliced leeks, it is easier to wash them after cutting. Drain thoroughly in a salad spinner or colander.

## recipe suggestions

Vichyssoise (potato leek soup) is the most famous leek preparation and a delicious one. In almost every case leeks can be substituted for onions. Take a hint from Europe where leeks are sometimes called "poor man's asparagus" and try them on their own. Braised or poached, leeks become silky and mild. They caramelize and become sweet when roasted or grilled.

# leek strudels

    Nonstick cooking spray
  2 pounds leeks, cleaned and sliced
      (white parts only)
  ¼ teaspoon caraway seeds
  ¼ teaspoon salt
  ⅛ teaspoon white pepper
  ¼ cup vegetable broth
  3 sheets frozen phyllo dough, thawed

1. Coat large skillet with cooking spray; heat over medium heat. Add leeks; cook and stir about 5 minutes or until tender. Stir in caraway seeds, salt and pepper. Add broth; bring to a boil over high heat. Reduce heat to low. Simmer, covered, about 5 minutes or until broth is absorbed. Cool to room temperature.

2. Preheat oven to 400°F. Cut each sheet of phyllo dough lengthwise into thirds. Spray one piece with cooking spray; spoon 2 tablespoons leek mixture near bottom of piece. Keep remaining phyllo covered with damp towel to prevent drying out. Fold one corner over filling to make triangle. Continue folding, as you would fold a flag, to make triangular packet.

3. Repeat with remaining phyllo dough and leek mixture. Place packets on ungreased baking sheet; lightly coat tops of packets with cooking spray. Bake about 20 minutes or until golden brown. Serve warm.

*Makes 9 servings*

## nutrients per serving:

**Calories** 81
**Calories from Fat** 7%
**Protein** 2g
**Carbohydrate** 18g
**Fiber** 2g

**Total Fat** 1g
**Saturated Fat** <1g
**Cholesterol** 0mg
**Sodium** 131mg

# Lemons

Tart, tangy lemons bring sunshine to our tables year round. A little squeeze brightens dishes both savory and sweet. So pucker up and get your vitamin C.

## benefits

Lemons are loaded with vitamin C, an antioxidant that helps fight heart disease, inflammation and cancer. Try a squeeze of lemon to brighten flavors in place of salt if you're watching your sodium. Even the aroma of lemons can perfume a room and lift your spirits.

## selection and storage

Lemons with thin skins that are heavy for their size will be the juiciest. Look for fruit without cuts, bruises or signs of mold. Lemons are available and harvested year round. Smaller, rounder Meyer lemons are sweeter and thought to be a cross between a lemon and an orange. Lemons will keep at room temperature for a week. They will last longer under refrigeration but will yield less juice when squeezed cold. Whole lemons cannot be frozen, but lemon juice freezes very well. Try filling an ice cube tray with lemon juice and then popping out the cubes as needed.

## preparation

If you need both juice and grated lemon peel (zest), grate the peel first. Wash the lemon well (if possible, use an unwaxed lemon). Grate the outer yellow part of the peel avoiding the bitter white pith underneath. You can use the small holes on a box grater, a flat grater or a zester. To get maximum juice from a lemon, have it at room temperature. You can microwave it for 15 seconds to warm it up if it's been refrigerated. Roll it back and forth on the counter firmly with the palm of your hand to loosen the juice sacs. Cut it in half and juice with a citrus juicer, reamer or just a squeeze of your hands.

## recipe suggestions

Grated lemon peel can add intensity to all sorts of baked goods. A tablespoon or two of lemon juice can be used to turn dairy-free milk into a buttermilk substitute. While lemon juice perks up the flavor of most vegetables, it will turn green ones an unappetizing drab olive color, so serve a wedge on the side for last minute squeezing.

# lemon-tossed linguine

8 ounces uncooked linguine pasta
   Grated peel and juice of 1 lemon,
    divided
2 teaspoons dairy-free margarine
2 tablespoons minced chives
⅓ cup dairy-free milk
1 teaspoon cornstarch
1 tablespoon minced fresh dill
1 tablespoon minced fresh parsley
¼ teaspoon white pepper
3 tablespoons grated dairy-free cheese
    alternative

1. Cook linguine according to package directions. Drain well. Place in medium bowl and sprinkle with lemon juice.

2. Meanwhile, melt margarine in small saucepan over medium heat. Add chives; cook until soft. Combine milk and cornstarch in small bowl; stir into saucepan. Cook and stir until thickened. Stir in dill, parsley, lemon peel and pepper.

3. Pour sauce over linguine. Sprinkle with dairy-free cheese; toss to coat evenly. Garnish with lemon slices and dill sprigs.

*Makes 3 servings*

## nutrients per serving:

| | |
|---|---|
| **Calories** 346 | **Total Fat** 4g |
| **Calories from Fat** 10% | **Saturated Fat** 1g |
| **Protein** 14g | **Cholesterol** 0mg |
| **Carbohydrate** 60g | **Sodium** 131mg |
| **Fiber** 3g | |

# Lentils

Like all legumes, lentils are good for you. Better yet, they require no soaking, cook relatively quickly and are very versatile. If you have lentils in your cupboard dinner is almost ready!

## benefits

Legumes are a class of vegetable that includes beans, peas and lentils, all of which grow in pods. (What about green beans? When the entire pod is eaten, the plant is considered a green vegetable.) Like other legumes, lentils make nutritious sense in a vegan diet because they are a good source of both protein and iron. Lentils are also rich in soluble fiber, which helps lower cholesterol and keep blood sugar steady. They have a mild, earthy taste that absorbs the flavor of what they are cooked with, especially spicy seasonings.

## selection and storage

Dried disc-shaped lentils come in a variety of colors—the most commonly available is a greenish-brown. Keep an eye out for French green lentils, black beluga lentils or the extremely quick cooking red lentils. Purchase lentils from a market with high turnover. For the widest selection, try an Indian market, where you'll find a huge variety of lentils, which are referred to as "dal." Choose lentils that look clean, dry and not dusty or shriveled. While they have a long shelf life, lentils are best used within a year. Store them in a cool, dry place. Canned lentils offer almost the same nutrition as dried and are readily available.

## preparation

There's no need to presoak lentils. Pick them over and remove any dirt or foreign particles, then rinse under cold water. Use about two cups of water or broth for each cup of lentils. Most varieties cook in 15 minutes to 45 minutes. Choose brown or green lentils if you want them to keep their shape. Red lentils become creamy and are best for preparations that require a smooth texture.

## recipe suggestions

Lentils make a hearty addition to soups, stews and chilis. A dish of lentils and rice is delicious and also provides complete protein. Cold lentils and vegetables make an excellent salad. Lentils are a staple in Indian cuisine, so check an ethnic cookbook for some great ideas.

# lentil rice curry

- 2 tablespoons olive oil
- 1 cup sliced green onions
- 3 cloves garlic, minced
- 2 tablespoons minced fresh ginger
- 2 teaspoons curry powder
- ½ teaspoon ground cumin
- ½ teaspoon ground turmeric
- 3 cups water
- 1 can (about 14 ounces) stewed tomatoes, undrained
- ½ teaspoon salt
- 1 cup uncooked red lentils, sorted and rinsed
- 1 large head cauliflower (about 1¼ pounds), broken into florets
- 1 tablespoon lemon juice
- Fragrant Basmati Rice (recipe follows, optional)

1. Heat oil in large saucepan over medium heat. Add onions, garlic, ginger, curry, cumin and turmeric; cook and stir 5 minutes. Add water, tomatoes and salt; bring to a boil over high heat.

2. Add lentils to saucepan. Reduce heat to low. Cover and simmer 20 to 30 minutes or until lentils are tender. Add cauliflower and lemon juice. Cover and simmer 8 to 10 minutes more or until cauliflower is tender.

3. Meanwhile prepare Fragrant Basmati Rice, if desired. Serve with lentil curry.

*Makes 6 servings*

## fragrant basmati rice

- 2 cups apple juice
- ¾ cup water
- ½ teaspoon salt
- 1½ cups basmati rice
- 2 thin slices fresh ginger
- 1 cinnamon stick (2 inches long)

Bring juice, water and salt to a boil in medium saucepan. Add remaining ingredients; reduce heat to low. Cover; simmer 25 to 30 minutes or until liquid is absorbed. Remove and discard ginger and cinnamon stick.     *Makes 4 cups*

## nutrients per serving:

| | |
|---|---|
| **Calories** 193 | **Total Fat** 5g |
| **Calories from Fat** 24% | **Saturated Fat** 1g |
| **Protein** 10g | **Cholesterol** 0mg |
| **Carbohydrate** 28g | **Sodium** 361mg |
| **Fiber** 12g | |

# Macadamia Nuts

Rich, buttery macadamia nuts are usually associated with Hawaii, but actually originated in Australia as an aboriginal delicacy. These luxurious tasting nuts are one of the best plant sources of omega-3 fatty acids.

## benefits

Macadamia nuts are high in fat and calories, but it is mostly good fat—the monounsaturated kind found in olive oil and believed to be beneficial in reducing cholesterol. They are also one of the very few plants to contain heart-healthy palmitoleic acid (also called omega-7). Like all nuts macadamias are high in protein and fiber. Macadamias' silky, smooth texture and mild slightly sweet taste add interest to vegan dishes both sweet and savory.

## selection and storage

You will always see shelled macadamia nuts since the shells are very difficult to crack. They were once much more expensive than other nuts, partly for this reason, but prices have come down as macadamias have become more popular and are cultivated in more places. They come raw, roasted, salted or unsalted. Choose nuts that are light in color without cracks. Because they are high in fat, macadamias can easily become rancid. Store unopened packages in the refrigerator for up to six months or the freezer for up to a year. Once opened, use macadamias within two months. If they develop an off odor or darken, discard them.

## preparation

To toast macadamias, spread them in a single layer on a baking pan and bake in a preheated 350°F oven for 10 to 15 minutes. Allow them to cool before grinding or chopping or they may become pasty. Grind macadamias in a food processor, but pulse carefully. The high oil content means they can quickly turn into nut butter. If you do accidentally overprocess, enjoy the macadamia butter as a delicious spread!

## recipe suggestions

Macadamia nuts can be substituted for other nuts in most recipes. They are delicious in desserts of all kinds and pair very well with chocolate and coconut. Ground macadamias have a creamy texture that makes them a good ingredient in pesto and other sauces and they are often included in vegan recipes for cheese substitutes.

# maui waui cookies

- 2 cups all-purpose flour
- 1 cup quick oats
- ½ teaspoon baking powder
- ½ teaspoon salt
- ½ teaspoon ground cinnamon
- ¼ teaspoon baking soda
- 1 cup sugar
- 1 cup (2 sticks) dairy-free margarine, softened
- Prepared egg replacer equal to 1 egg
- ¾ cup coarsely chopped salted macadamia nuts
- ½ cup packed shredded coconut
- Pineapple Glaze (recipe follows, optional)

1. Preheat oven to 400°F. Line cookie sheets with parchment paper. Combine flour, oats, baking powder, salt, cinnamon and baking soda in medium bowl.

2. Beat margarine and sugar in large bowl with electric mixer at medium-high speed until fluffy. Beat in egg replacer. Gradually beat in flour mixture until well blended. Mix in macadamia nuts and coconut.

3. Drop dough by heaping tablespoonfuls 2 inches apart onto prepared cookie sheets. Bake 12 to 16 minutes or until cookies are set and edges are highly browned.

4. Cool on cookie sheets 2 minutes. Slide parchment paper with cookies to wire rack; cool completely. Prepare Pineapple Glaze, if desired; drizzle over cookies.

*Makes about 3 dozen cookies*

**Pineapple Glaze:** Place 1 cup powdered sugar in medium bowl. Gradually stir in 4 to 6 teaspoons unsweetened pineapple juice until glaze is consistency for drizzling.

## nutrients per serving:

**Calories** 124
**Calories from Fat** 54%
**Protein** 1g
**Carbohydrate** 13g
**Fiber** 1g
**Total Fat** 8g
**Saturated Fat** 3g
**Cholesterol** 0mg
**Sodium** 109mg

# Mangoes

There's no other fruit like the mango. Its fragrance and unique tropical sweetness are difficult to describe and impossible to resist. No wonder it is often called the king of fruits.

## benefits

For thousands of years, the mango has been cultivated in Southeast Asia where it is revered as a symbol of love and life. Some even believe the mango tree can grant wishes. Those benefits are unproven, but the king of fruits definitely rules when it comes to providing vitamin C—one mango has an entire day's worth. Mangoes are also a superior source of beta-carotene and contribute significant amounts of calcium, potassium, magnesium and fiber. In addition, mangoes contain an enzyme that aids digestion.

## selection and storage

There are more than 200 varieties of mangoes with colors ranging from yellow to bright red and orange. The most commonly available variety is the Tommy Atkins, but be sure to try the golden Ataulfo mango (sometimes called Manila or Philippine mango) when you see it. This variety is very rich in flavor and much less fibrous than the larger Tommy Atkins. Choose mangoes that yield to gentle pressure with smooth skin and no dark spots or bruises. Your nose is the best judge of ripeness—a mango should be very fragrant. Mango is also available canned or frozen.

## preparation

The tricky part of preparing a mango is cutting the flesh away from the long flat pit in the center. The thicker part of mango flesh is on the flatter sides of the mango, which is counterintuitive. Stand the mango on end and slice the fruit from stem to tip, coming as close as you can to the pit. Lay each mango half skin side down and score the flesh in a crosshatch pattern without cutting through the skin. Then bend the piece inside out. The cubes of mango flesh will pop up and be easy to slice away provided you can resist nibbling them then and there.

## recipe suggestions

Frozen mango pieces are great whirred into a smoothie. Mango salsa is a delightful accompaniment to chips, grilled tofu or a grain dish like couscous or brown rice.

## quinoa and mango salad

- 1 cup uncooked quinoa*
- 2 cups water
- 2 cups cubed peeled mango (about 2 large mangoes)
- ½ cup sliced green onions
- ½ cup dried cranberries
- 2 tablespoons chopped fresh parsley
- ¼ cup olive oil
- 1 tablespoon plus 1½ teaspoons white wine vinegar
- 1 teaspoon Dijon mustard
- ½ teaspoon salt
- ⅛ teaspoon black pepper

*See page 140 for more information.

1. Place quinoa in fine-mesh strainer; rinse well under cold running water. Transfer to medium saucepan and add water. Bring to a boil. Reduce heat; simmer, covered, 10 to 12 minutes until water is absorbed. Fluff with fork. Transfer to large bowl; cover and refrigerate at least 1 hour.

2. Add mango, green onions, cranberries and parsley to quinoa; mix well.

3. Combine oil, vinegar, mustard, salt and pepper in small bowl; whisk until blended. Pour over salad; toss to combine.

*Makes 8 (⅔-cup) servings*

**Tip:** This salad can be made several hours ahead and refrigerated. Allow it to stand at room temperature for at least 30 minutes before serving.

### nutrients per serving:

| | |
|---|---|
| **Calories** 200 | **Total Fat** 8g |
| **Calories from Fat** 37% | **Saturated Fat** 1g |
| **Protein** 3g | **Cholesterol** 0mg |
| **Carbohydrate** 30g | **Sodium** 172mg |
| **Fiber** 3g | |

# Meatless Sausage

There are times we need something to toss on the grill or add an extra oomph to a pot of beans or rice. Meatless sausages fill the bill in a variety of flavors and forms.

## benefits

Meatless sausage is usually made primarily of soy. Unlike a meat-based sausage, it contains heart-healthy polyunsaturated and/or monounsaturated fats instead of artery-clogging saturated fat. Most vegetarian and vegan sausages contain fewer calories than ordinary sausage and since soy is one of the few plant sources of complete protein, you'll also be getting all your essential amino acids. Check labels carefully, however, as some meatless products contain eggs or dairy and aren't suitable for vegans. Some also use fillers you may wish to avoid.

## selection and storage

Today there are a huge number of choices in meatless sausage. Spices are what give sausages their unique flavor profiles and you can now enjoy meatless versions of hot dogs, breakfast sausages, bratwurst, Italian sausage and more. In addition to sausage links (don't worry, the casings are made of plant fibers), sausage patties and bulk sausage are available, so choose according to the recipe you're using. The main consideration will probably be the ingredients in the product. In addition to soy, meatless sausages may be made with mushrooms, nuts, beans, seitan or a combination of vegetables.

## preparation

While the ingredients in a meatless sausage may not need cooking for food safety reasons, these sausages do need to be cooked to achieve the proper texture and flavor. Heating gelatinizes the starch to make a firm, plump sausage. Check the package directions for each individual product. Frozen sausage may need to be thawed first and optimum flavor depends on following directions based on the ingredients and processing of the product.

## recipe suggestions

Meatless sausage opens a whole world of possibilities to the vegan. Protein at breakfast is now an easy option. Want a filling for tacos? Use a loose sausage product or break patties up into pieces in a skillet and add the desired seasonings. Vegetarian pepperoni tastes a lot like the real thing and you can probably serve it on pizza and even fool the meat eaters in the crowd.

# vegetarian sausage rice

- 2 cups chopped green bell peppers
- 1 can (about 15 ounces) dark red kidney beans, rinsed and drained
- 1 can (about 14 ounces) diced tomatoes with green bell peppers and onions
- 1 cup chopped onion
- 1 cup sliced celery
- 1 cup water, divided
- ¾ cup uncooked long grain white rice
- 1¼ teaspoons salt
- 1 teaspoon hot pepper sauce
- ½ teaspoon dried thyme
- ½ teaspoon red pepper flakes
- 3 bay leaves
- 1 package (about 8 ounces) meatless breakfast patties, thawed
- 2 tablespoons extra virgin olive oil
- ½ cup chopped fresh parsley

## Slow Cooker Directions

1. Combine bell peppers, beans, tomatoes, onion, celery, ½ cup water, rice, salt, hot pepper sauce, thyme, red pepper flakes and bay leaves in slow cooker. Cover; cook on LOW 4 to 5 hours. Remove and discard bay leaves.

2. Dice breakfast patties. Heat oil in large skillet over medium-high heat. Add sausage; cook 2 minutes or until lightly browned. Transfer sausage to slow cooker.

3. Add remaining ½ cup water to skillet; bring to a boil over high heat and cook 1 minute, scraping up browned bits from skillet. Add liquid and parsley to slow cooker; stir gently to blend. *Makes 8 servings*

## nutrients per serving:

| | |
|---|---|
| **Calories** 228 | **Total Fat** 7g |
| **Calories from Fat** 26% | **Saturated Fat** 1g |
| **Protein** 11g | **Cholesterol** 0mg |
| **Carbohydrate** 33g | **Sugar** 0g |
| **Fiber** 8g | **Sodium** 891mg |

# Millet

Amazing millet is a forgotten grain. These tiny little seeds have been making big contributions to cuisines in Asia and Africa since ancient times. Discover millet's mild, nutty flavor and versatility for yourself.

## benefits

Millet seeds may be small, but they pack a big serving of vitamins, minerals and fiber. (Strictly speaking millet is a seed, not a grain.) Gluten-free millet provides

about as much protein as wheat, along with niacin, vitamin B$_6$, folic acid, potassium and magnesium. Millet's flavor is delicate enough to take on the character of what it is cooked with and depending on how it's cooked, millet can be crunchy, fluffy or creamy.

## selection and storage

Unless you have a beak, you'll need to purchase hulled millet. The millet used as birdseed isn't suitable for human consumption. No worries though, since the millet you'll find in supermarkets and health food stores is sold hulled. Millet is most often found in bulk bins. Choose a store with a high turnover and take a sniff of the grain—it should not smell musty. Millet has a fairly long shelf life. Keep it dry and cool and store in an airtight container for up to a year in the cupboard. For longer storage, refrigerate or freeze millet. Millet can also be purchased ground into flour.

## preparation

To prepare millet as a cereal or side dish, simmer it in the liquid of your choice in a ratio of three parts liquid to one part millet. For a fluffy result, leave it alone as it cooks. It will be done in about 25 minutes. If you stir the millet while it cooks and add additional water as needed, you'll end up with a creamy texture resembling mashed potatoes. Toasting millet before cooking brings out its nutty flavor. You can even pop millet like popcorn.

## recipe suggestions

Cooked millet is an excellent breakfast cereal with added fruit or nuts and some dairy-free milk. It can be also be served instead of rice or couscous and used in casseroles and stuffings. Raw millet adds a nice crunch when added to the batter for baked goods.

## millet pilaf

- 1 tablespoon olive oil
- ½ onion, finely chopped
- ½ red bell pepper, finely chopped
- 1 carrot, finely chopped
- 2 cloves garlic, minced
- 1 cup uncooked millet
- 3 cups water
- Grated peel and juice from 1 lemon
- ¾ teaspoon salt
- ¼ teaspoon black pepper
- 2 tablespoons chopped fresh parsley (optional)

1. Heat oil in medium saucepan over medium heat. Add onion, bell pepper, carrot and garlic; cook and stir 5 minutes or until softened. Add millet; cook and stir 5 minutes or until lightly toasted.

2. Stir in water, lemon peel and juice, salt and black pepper; bring to a boil. Reduce heat to low; cover and simmer 30 minutes or until water is absorbed and millet is tender. Let stand, covered, 5 minutes. Fluff with fork. Sprinkle with parsley, if desired.

*Makes 6 servings*

## nutrients per serving:

| | | |
|---|---|---|
| **Calories** 164 | **Carbohydrate** 28g | **Saturated Fat** 1g |
| **Calories from Fat** 22% | **Fiber** 4g | **Cholesterol** 0mg |
| **Protein** 4g | **Total Fat** 4g | **Sodium** 304mg |

# Miso

Miso is a fermented soy-based seasoning paste with a smooth, buttery texture and a tangy, salty taste. Japanese miso soup is the most common use, but miso is also used for dressings, marinades and sauces.

## benefits

The Japanese start most mornings with a bowl of miso soup. Its health-giving properties are said to include improving digestion, protecting from cancer and even helping remove toxins from exposure to heavy metals or radiation. Not all those claims are proven, but it is true that a single tablespoon of miso contains 2 grams of protein and has only 25 calories. It brings a rich, savory flavor to vegetable and grain dishes. All in all, marvelous miso is a must for vegan diets.

## selection and storage

Most miso is made from soybeans, though there are also types made from barley and rice. A yeast mold called "koji" is added and fermentation time can be from a few weeks to years. The color and texture depend on the ingredients and fermentation time and the Japanese consider the making of miso an art akin to cheese making. You'll find miso in tightly sealed plastic or glass containers in health food stores and some supermarkets. Shiromiso, the most common and sweetest variety, is a golden-yellow color and is also called "white" miso. Darker colored misos have a more intense flavor. Miso is most often used to make soup, which is traditionally prepared with dashi, a fish stock. Some miso may have dashi added to it, so check labels. Store miso, tightly sealed, in the refrigerator where it will keep for up to a year.

## preparation

To make a vegan miso soup, heat water and miso paste over medium-low heat and stir to dissolve. Do not boil. Miso can also be used as an ingredient in many salad dressings with the addition of oil and perhaps some orange juice, ginger and garlic.

## recipe suggestions

Miso is quite salty and can be used instead of salt to add a much more complex depth of flavor to many dishes. It is also a good thickener for sauces and stews and can be used, as is, as a spread on crackers or sandwiches.

## miso soup with tofu

- 4 cups water
- 1 tablespoon shredded nori or wakame seaweed
- 8 ounces firm tofu, cut into ½-inch cubes (about 1½ cups)
- 3 green onions, finely chopped
- ¼ cup white miso
- 2 teaspoons soy sauce

1. Bring water to a simmer in medium saucepan and add nori. Simmer 6 minutes.

2. Reduce heat to low and add remaining ingredients. Stir until miso is dissolved and soup is heated through. Do not boil.

*Makes 4 (1-cup) servings*

# Molasses

Get stuck on molasses instead of the empty calories of refined sugar or fake sweeteners. Molasses has a naturally complex, bittersweet flavor and is actually good for you.

## benefits

Molasses is what's leftover after refining white sugar, so it's a concentrated source of the minerals that have been removed. It's a very good source of iron and calcium, which are both important in vegan diets where these nutrients can be more difficult to obtain. All molasses is nutritionally superior to refined sugar and blackstrap molasses is the most nutrient dense and least sweet variety. It is the syrup remaining after the third boiling of sugar extraction; light and medium and dark molasses are from the first and second processing.

## selection and storage

Jars of light and dark molasses are usually found near the pancake syrups in the supermarket. For blackstrap molasses, you may need to visit a health food store. Look for the word "unsulphured" on the label, which means no sulphur was used in extraction. Unsulphured molasses has a lighter, cleaner flavor. Blackstrap molasses is something of an acquired taste since it has definite bitter overtones. You may want to reserve it for savory dishes or those with other strong flavors. Molasses should be stored in a cool, dark place and will retain its quality for up to two years. Wipe the lid clean after each use. If mold appears, discard the entire jar.

## preparation

Molasses is very sticky stuff! Before measuring, spray cups with nonstick cooking spray and molasses will slip out more easily and cleanup will be a breeze. If you wish to substitute molasses for white sugar, you will need to reduce other liquid in the recipe to compensate (³/₄ cup sugar plus ¹/₄ cup of water equals 1 cup of molasses). Molasses can also cause baked goods to darken more quickly so the oven temperature may need to be slightly reduced.

## recipe suggestions

Gingerbread and baked beans are two classic uses for molasses. It also works as a seasoning for collards or other greens and as an ingredient in chili or barbecue sauce. Besides being delicious in cookies, molasses can add a welcome touch of sweetness to whole grain breads or crackers.

# ginger molasses cookies

- 1 cup shortening
- 1 cup granulated sugar
- 1 tablespoon baking soda
- 2 teaspoons ground ginger
- 2 teaspoons ground cinnamon
- ½ teaspoon ground nutmeg
- ½ teaspoon ground cloves
- ½ teaspoon salt
- 1 cup molasses
- ⅔ cup double-strength instant coffee*
  Prepared egg replacer equal to 1 egg
- 4¾ cups all-purpose flour

*To prepare double-strength coffee, follow instructions for instant coffee but use twice the recommended amount of instant coffee granules.*

**1.** Preheat oven to 350°F. Lightly grease cookie sheets.

**2.** Beat shortening and sugar in large bowl with electric mixer until creamy. Beat in baking soda, ginger, cinnamon, nutmeg, cloves and salt until well blended. Add molasses, coffee and egg replacer, beating well after each addition. Gradually add flour, beating at low speed just until blended.

**3.** Drop dough by tablespoonfuls 2 inches apart onto prepared cookie sheets. Bake 12 to 15 minutes or until cookies are set but not browned. Cool on cookie sheets 1 minute. Remove to wire racks; cool completely.

*Makes about 4 dozen cookies*

## nutrients per serving:

**Calories** 118
**Calories from Fat** 32%
**Protein** 1g
**Carbohydrate** 19g
**Fiber** <1g
**Total Fat** 4g
**Saturated Fat** 1g
**Cholesterol** 0mg
**Sodium** 106mg

# Mustard Greens

With lime green or purple-red leaves that can be curly or flat, mustard greens come in an many shapes and sizes. Cute baby leaves spice up a salad and larger ones add zest to a soup, grain or side dish.

## benefits

Mustard greens are cruciferous vegetables like cabbage and brussels sprouts and they share much of the same good nutrition. They are rich in vitamin C, vitamin E and beta-carotene, cancer-fighting antioxidants. They are also a good source of vitamin K, vitamin E, vitamin B6, folic acid, calcium and fiber. It might be easier to list the nutrients they don't have!

If that weren't enough, mustard greens are also very low in calories—only 20 in a cup.

## selection and storage

All mustard greens have a spicy bite and sometimes a touch of bitterness as well. Small reddish leaves are frequently one of the salad greens in a mesclun mix and it's best to choose small young leaves if you plan to eat them raw. Larger leaves are sold bundled in bunches. The most common variety is medium green with ruffled leaves and may be labeled curled mustard or simply "greens." There are also red and purple mustards and several Asian varieties. For all sorts, choose bunches with a bright color and no dry or yellow leaves. Store in the refrigerator no more than a few days wrapped in ventilated plastic. Mustard greens are also available frozen.

## preparation

Like all greens, mustard greens must be well washed. Swish the leaves around in water and lift them out so sand and dirt fall to the bottom. Large leaves should be stemmed. Fold the leaf and grasp the bottom of the stem and pull it toward the leaf tip to remove it. Since even the same kinds of mustard greens can vary greatly in pungency, it's wise to taste one before cooking to determine the best method. Boiling will reduce the sharp bite; wilting or steaming will preserve it.

## recipe suggestions

Mustard greens have an earthy spiciness that works well with bland foods like potatoes, rice, pasta, corn and beans. A little sweetness in the form of balsamic vinegar or dried coconut is a nice addition to sautéed greens.

# garlicky mustard greens

- 2 pounds mustard greens
- 1 teaspoon olive oil
- 1 cup chopped onion
- 2 cloves garlic, minced
- ¾ cup chopped red bell pepper
- ½ cup reduced-sodium vegetable broth
- 1 tablespoon cider vinegar
- 1 teaspoon sugar

**1.** Remove stems and any wilted leaves from greens. Stack several leaves; roll up. Cut crosswise into 1-inch slices. Repeat with remaining greens.

**2.** Heat oil in large saucepan over medium heat. Add onion and garlic; cook and stir 5 minutes or until onion is tender. Stir in greens, bell pepper and broth. Reduce heat to low. Cover and cook 25 minutes or until greens are tender, stirring occasionally.

**3.** Combine vinegar and sugar in small bowl; stir until sugar is dissolved. Stir into greens; remove from heat. Serve immediately.

*Makes 4 servings*

## nutrients per serving:

| | |
|---|---|
| **Calories** 72 | **Total Fat** 2g |
| **Calories from Fat** 0% | **Saturated Fat** <1g |
| **Protein** 6g | **Cholesterol** 0mg |
| **Carbohydrate** 11g | **Sodium** 42mg |
| **Fiber** 5g | |

# Nori

Nori is the seaweed best known as a sushi wrapper. Like other sea vegetables, it provides a unique and beneficial mineral content that cannot be found in plants grown in the soil.

## benefits

Nori takes its nutrients from the sea, making it rich in minerals including iron, calcium, potassium, magnesium, selenium and iodine. It also contains vitamin C, which makes iron easier for the body to absorb. Considered a health food for thousands of years in Japan, nori is also high in fiber and protein. It requires no cooking and has a mild taste of the sea along with a delightful crisp texture.

## selection and storage

Nori—also called laver—comes in paper-like sheets. It is made from fresh seaweed, which is washed and chopped, then spread into sheets and dried. You will find it in the Asian section of the supermarket, or for an eye-opening look at the many kinds of nori and other sea vegetables, visit a Japanese or Korean market. Nori almost always comes toasted. Untoasted nori is purplish black, but toasted it develops a slight shiny green cast. Look for packages that are tightly sealed with unbroken sheets. Store unopened packages of nori in a cool, dry place for up to six months. Once opened, transfer to an airtight food storage bag and use it as soon as possible. Humidity of any kind is an enemy of nori, so do not refrigerate it.

## preparation

If you need to toast nori, simply pass the sheet over a flame a few times. To use nori as a sushi wrap, you'll need a simple bamboo rolling mat. They are inexpensive and can be purchased at housewares stores or Asian markets. Line the mat with plastic wrap, place the nori on the wrap and arrange rice and fillings. Use the mat to roll the ingredients together tightly.

## recipe suggestions

In addition to using nori as a sushi wrap, use crumbled nori as a topping for rice. Add strips of nori to salads or soups, especially miso soup. To make healthy nori "chips", brush sheets of nori with dark sesame oil, sprinkle with salt and bake in a 400°F oven until crisp, about 10 minutes. Cool and cut into strips.

# vegetarian sushi maki

- **4 to 6 sheets toasted sushi nori**
- **1 teaspoon wasabi**
- **1½ cups Sushi Rice (recipe follows)**
- **1 ripe avocado, thinly sliced**
- **4 thin strips peeled cucumber**
- **¼ cup loosely packed spinach leaves, thinly sliced**
- **½ cup thinly sliced carrot, steamed**
- **4 teaspoons toasted sesame seeds**
  **Pickled ginger and soy sauce (optional)**

1. Place one sheet of nori on rolling mat. Cover bottom third of sheet with thin layer of wasabi. Spread about ⅓ cup rice on top of wasabi, leaving an inch uncovered along bottom edge. Distribute one quarter each of avocado, cucumber, spinach, carrot and sesame seeds on top of rice.

2. Moisten top edge of nori sheet. Lift bottom edge; press it into rice, rolling rice into nori as you would a jelly-roll until it is folded over to top edge. Press gently to seal. Repeat with remaining ingredients.

3. Cut rolls into 1-inch slices with sharp knife, wiping knife with warm water if it gets sticky. Serve with pickled ginger and soy sauce.

*Makes 6 to 8 rolls*

## sushi rice

- **1¾ cups water**
- **½ teaspoon salt**
- **1 cup uncooked sushi rice**
- **⅓ cup seasoned rice vinegar**

1. Bring water and salt to a boil in medium saucepan. Stir in rice; reduce heat to a low. Simmer, covered, 20 minutes or until water is absorbed.

2. Remove from heat; let stand 5 minutes. Transfer rice to shallow bowl; let cool slightly. Sprinkle with vinegar and stir gently.

*Makes 2 cups*

## nutrients per serving:

**Calories** 67
**Calories from Fat** 0%
**Protein** 2g
**Carbohydrate** 12g
**Fiber** 1g
**Total Fat** 1g
**Saturated Fat** 0g
**Cholesterol** 0mg
**Sodium** 0mg

# Nutritional Yeast

This magical ingredient has a nutty, cheesy flavor that is a favorite with many vegans. Nutritional yeast adds a savory something to many recipes and can be sprinkled on popcorn or pasta like Parmesan cheese.

## benefits

Nutritional yeast is an inactive version of yeast. (It won't make bread rise or expand in your tummy.) If you're a full-time vegan, it's a good idea to make it part of your diet. One rounded tablespoon will provide you with a heaping helping of B-complex vitamins, including several days worth of thiamin, riboflavin, niacin, $B_6$ and $B_{12}$. In fact, it is the only reliable food source of vitamin $B_{12}$. (Check labels, however. Most, but not ALL, nutritional yeast has $B_{12}$.) It is also a plant-based way to get umami, the savory flavor that many miss when they eliminate cheese from their diets.

## selection and storage

Nutritional yeast, which is sometimes called vegetarian yeast, is sold in a powder or flake form. It is yellowish and looks a bit like cornstarch. It is not the same thing as regular yeast for bread or brewer's yeast, which has a much harsher flavor and different nutrients. You'll find nutritional yeast in health food stores, natural foods stores and online. While all nutritional yeast is rich in B vitamins, vitamin $B_{12}$ is only present in fortified forms, so check labels. Store nutritional yeast in a sealed container away from light and moisture at room temperature. It should stay fresh for up to a year.

## preparation

Nutritional yeast can be used as a condiment and sprinkled on popcorn, garlic bread and salads. You may want to keep a small amount available in a shaker jar at the table as they do in some vegetarian restaurants.

In addition, nutritional yeast is a necessary ingredient in many recipes for cheese replacements.

## recipe suggestions

Nutritional yeast is the healthy vegan cheese substitute. It is used in countless recipes, including those for cheese sauces, pastas, gravies, tofu and meatless patties. To make a dairy-free "parmesan" sprinkle for pizza, salad or vegetables, combine equal parts almonds, nutritional yeast and bread crumbs in a food processor; pulse to combine and add salt to taste.

# scrambled tofu skillet

- 5 tablespoons olive oil, divided
- 4 red potatoes, cubed
- ½ white onion, sliced
- 1 tablespoon chopped fresh rosemary
- 1 teaspoon coarse salt
- ¼ cup nutritional yeast
- ½ teaspoon turmeric
- 2 tablespoons water
- 2 tablespoons soy sauce
- 1 package (14 ounces) firm tofu, cut into 8 cubes
- ½ cup chopped green bell pepper
- ½ cup chopped red onion
- 2 green onions, chopped

1. Preheat oven to 450°F. Place 2 tablespoons oil in 12-inch cast-iron skillet; place skillet in oven 10 minutes before ready to bake potatoes.

2. Bring large saucepan of water to a boil. Add potatoes; cook 5 to 7 minutes or until potatoes are tender. Drain and return to saucepan; stir in white onion, 2 tablespoons oil, rosemary and salt. Spread mixture in preheated skillet. Bake 25 to 30 minutes or until potatoes are browned, stirring every 10 minutes and adding additional oil, if needed.

3. Combine nutritional yeast and turmeric in small bowl. Stir in water and soy sauce until blended. Squeeze water from tofu cubes and coarsely crumble tofu into large bowl.

4. Heat remaining 1 tablespoon oil in large skillet over medium-high heat. Add green pepper and red onion; cook and stir 2 minutes or until softened. Add tofu and 3 tablespoons sauce mixture. Cook and stir 5 minutes or until liquid is evaporated and tofu is heated through. Stir in additional sauce, if desired. Serve over potatoes and sprinkle with green onions.

*Makes 4 servings*

## nutrients per serving:

**Calories** 357
**Calories from Fat** 34%
**Protein** 15g
**Carbohydrate** 43g
**Fiber** 6g
**Total Fat** 13g
**Saturated Fat** 3g
**Cholesterol** 0mg
**Sodium** 1,176mg

# Oats

Are you feeling your oats? Whether instant, old-fashioned or steel-cut, oats are the whole grain almost everyone loves. They add good nutrition and fiber to meals from breakfast to dessert.

## benefits

Need to lower your cholesterol or risk of diabetes? Better eat more oats. The soluble fiber in two cups of oatmeal enjoyed every day has been shown to reduce cholesterol in only three months. A special type of soluble fiber called beta-glucan is largely responsible for this effect. Beta-glucan also helps keep your blood sugar under control by slowing sugar absorption. Even processed oat products like quick-cooking oats retain their fiber and nutrition. Although all oats are hulled, this does not strip away their bran and germ as it does with most other grains.

## selection and storage

Oats are readily available in many forms and can be purchased packaged or from bulk bins. Old-fashioned oats have a flat shape because they are steamed and rolled. Steel-cut oats or Irish oats are sliced into small pieces but not flattened. They take substantially longer to cook and have a chewy texture that many people love. Instant oatmeal is precooked and only needs to have boiling water added. It is still nutritious, but many flavored versions contain added sugar and salt. Oat bran is the outer layer of the oat grain. It is intact in all oats, but may also be purchased as a separate, stand-alone product. Store oats in an airtight container in a cool, dry place for up to one year. Oat flour is also available and may be combined with wheat flour when making bread.

## preparation

Breakfast oatmeal can be as simple as adding boiling water to precooked oats. To enjoy longer cooking steel-cut oats on a weekday morning, try preparing them overnight in a slow cooker. And don't forget to add fruit, nuts and a drizzle of maple syrup or molasses.

## recipe suggestions

Add oats to homemade veggie burgers for good nutrition. Oats can replace some of the flour in pancakes and breads. Grind oats to a powder in a blender or food processor and use to thicken soups or sauces.

# basic oatmeal cookies

- **2 cups old-fashioned oats**
- **1⅓ cups all-purpose flour**
- **1 teaspoon ground cinnamon**
- **¾ teaspoon baking soda**
- **½ teaspoon baking powder**
- **½ teaspoon salt**
- **½ teaspoon cornstarch\* (optional)**
- **1 cup packed light brown sugar**
- **¾ cup (1½ sticks) dairy-free margarine, softened**
- **½ cup granulated sugar**
- **¼ cup silken tofu, blended until smooth**

*\*Adding cornstarch will make the cookies a bit less puffy when baked.*

**1.** Preheat oven to 350°F. Combine oats, flour, cinnamon, baking soda, baking powder, salt and cornstarch, if desired, in medium bowl.

**2.** Beat brown sugar, margarine and granulated sugar in large bowl with electric mixer at medium speed until light and fluffy. Add tofu; beat until blended. Gradually add oat mixture, beating just until blended. Drop dough by tablespoonfuls 2 inches apart onto cookie sheets.

**3.** Bake 11 to 15 minutes or until puffed and golden. Cool 5 minutes on cookie sheets. Remove to wire racks; cool completely.

*Makes 3 dozen cookies*

## nutrients per serving:

**Calories** 110
**Calories from Fat** 34%
**Protein** 1g
**Carbohydrate** 17g
**Fiber** 1g
**Total Fat** 4g
**Saturated Fat** 2g

**Cholesterol** 0mg
**Sodium** 108mg

# Olive Oil

Who needs butter when there's delicious, healthy olive oil? No other oil adds such richness and flavor to vegetable dishes or tastes good enough to enjoy as a dip with bread.

## benefits

All oils are fats, but olive oil is very high in monounsaturated fatty acids (sometimes referred to as MUFAs). Vegans are ahead of the game since they eat few of the least healthy fats—the saturated kind—found mostly in animal products. A diet high in MUFAs may help lower your risk of heart disease by lowering cholesterol. Extra virgin olive oil is also an incredible source of polyphenols. These nutrients work as antioxidants and anti-inflammatory agents in the body.

## selection and storage

Now that olive oil has become popular, choosing the right type can be confusing. Extra virgin and virgin olive oil are from the first pressing of olives and are the most flavorful, least acidic and most healthful. No heat, solvent or chemicals may be used in the processing. Oil labeled "pure olive oil", or just "olive oil", is generally a blend of refined olive oil and virgin oil. "Light" olive oil has been processed to give it a more neutral flavor, but all olive oils have the same number of calories. Expensive extra virgin olive oil has a delicate flavor that can be compromised by high heat, so it isn't a good choice for frying. Store olive oil in a dark container away from light and heat, which can cause it to become rancid. Refrigerating olive oil will cause it to become cloudy, but it will return to normal at room temperature.

## preparation

Use olive oil as a condiment as well as an ingredient. While you can sauté in olive oil, the flavor really shines when it's added to cooked dishes. Drizzle it over steamed vegetables or cooked grains. In Italy, a few drops of extra virgin olive oil are often used to top pizza just before serving.

## recipe suggestions

Olive oil is incredibly versatile. Use it in place of butter for luscious mashed potatoes or as flavor enhancer for roasted vegetables. Of course, pasta, garlic, tomatoes and olive oil are made for each other.

# beans and greens crostini

- 4 tablespoons olive oil, divided
- 1 small onion, thinly sliced
- 4 cups thinly sliced kale (preferably Tuscan or dinosaur kale)*
- 2 tablespoons minced garlic, divided
- 1 tablespoon balsamic vinegar
- 2 teaspoons salt, divided
- ¼ teaspoon red pepper flakes
- 1 can (about 15 ounces) cannellini beans, rinsed and drained
- 1 tablespoon chopped fresh rosemary
  Toasted baguette slices

*See page 92 for more information.

1. Heat 1 tablespoon oil in large nonstick skillet. Add onion; cook and stir 5 minutes or until softened. Add kale and 1 tablespoon garlic; cook and stir 15 minutes or until kale is softened and most of liquid has evaporated. Stir in balsamic vinegar, 1 teaspoon salt and red pepper flakes.

2. Meanwhile, combine beans, remaining 3 tablespoons olive oil, 1 tablespoon garlic, rosemary and remaining 1 teaspoon salt in food processor; process until smooth paste forms.

3. Spread baguette slices with bean mixture; top with kale.          *Makes about 24 crostini*

## nutrients per serving:

**Calories** 44
**Calories from Fat** 48%
**Protein** 1g
**Carbohydrate** 4g
**Fiber** 1g
**Total Fat** 2g
**Saturated Fat** <1g
**Cholesterol** 0mg
**Sodium** 240mg

# Olives

Nature outdid herself with the olive—so much flavor in such a small package. Olives have been enjoyed since 3,000 BC and have always been a symbol of peace and wisdom.

## benefits

The nutritional benefits of olive oil are well recognized, but let's not forget that the olives it comes from are superstars in their own right. They are a rich source of monounsaturated fats that lower cholesterol. There are hundreds of types of olives and dozens of ways to cure them. The good news is that while they each have a unique nutritional profile, they all offer abundant antioxidant and anti-inflammatory benefits.

## selection and storage

Almost all olives are bitter when they are picked and must be cured or brined to mellow their flavor. Black olives are generally riper than green olives, but color also depends on curing. Olives are sold in jars or cans, but it's more fun to purchase from bulk bins or "olive bars" where you can sample new varieties and buy just what you need. Choose from Greek oil-cured kalamata, petite French niçoise, large meaty Italian Cerignola, and many more. You will also find olives flavored with herbs or stuffed with peppers, garlic or almonds. Pitted olives are handy for turning into tapenade or pasta sauce. Always select olives that are fairly firm, not mushy. Olives should be refrigerated in their own liquid in a non-metal container and will keep for several weeks.

## preparation

To pit olives, place them on a cutting board and lightly crush them with the flat side of a large knife. Slip the pit out of the cracked olive. To add interest to olives that will be served as an appetizer, marinate them with fresh herb sprigs, garlic, citrus juice and extra virgin olive oil.

## recipe suggestions

Both green and black olives make delicious tapenades to be used as a dip or spread. Combine pitted olives with garlic, capers, lemon juice, olive oil and herbs in a food processor and whir until a coarse paste is formed. Olives add interest to vegetable dishes of all kinds and pair particularly well with cauliflower, white beans and eggplant. Olives and oranges make a simple but delicious salad.

## pasta with fresh tomato-olive sauce

2 tablespoons olive oil
1 small onion, chopped
2 cloves garlic, minced
4 large ripe tomatoes, seeded and chopped (about 3 cups)
¾ teaspoon dried oregano
⅛ teaspoon red pepper flakes
⅔ cup chopped pitted kalamata olives
1 tablespoon capers
    Salt and black pepper
1 package (16 ounces) uncooked spaghetti
    Shredded dairy-free cheese alternative

1. Heat oil in large skillet over medium heat. Add onion and garlic; cook and stir about 4 minutes or until onion is tender.

2. Add tomatoes, oregano and red pepper flakes; simmer, uncovered, 15 to 20 minutes or until sauce is thickened. Stir in olives, capers, salt and black pepper.

3. Meanwhile, cook pasta according to package directions; drain. Add pasta to skillet; toss to coat with sauce. Sprinkle with cheese alternative. *Makes 6 to 8 servings*

### nutrients per serving:

Calories 362
Calories from Fat 19%
Protein 11g
Carbohydrate 63g
Fiber 4g
Total Fat 7g
Saturated Fat 1g
Cholesterol 0mg
Sodium 117mg

# Onions

Onions can taste sweet or spicy and their texture can be crisp and crunchy or soft and yielding. Onions lend their versatile flavor to so many dishes and yet rarely have a starring role. It's enough to bring a tear to your eye.

## benefits

Onions are part of the Allium family like garlic and share many of the same health benefits. Around the world and throughout history, onions have been believed to help fight colds and coughs. They contain sulfides, the compounds that can make you cry, but can also help lower cholesterol. Onions also contain phytonutrients that fight inflammation and may help to ward off chronic diseases. But onions add such flavor and depth to all sorts of recipes, their benefits extend far beyond the fact that they are good for you!

## selection and storage

Bulb onions can be red, yellow or white. Spring and summer onions have a lighter colored, thinner skin. Specialty sweet onions are part of this category. Fall and winter onions, sometimes called storage onions, have thicker skins and a longer shelf life. Look for onions that are firm with dry outer skins and no soft spots or dark patches. Store them in a space that's well ventilated away from heat, light and potatoes. A chemical reaction between onions and potatoes will cause them both to spoil more quickly. Yellow onions will keep for up to a month. Sweet onions are much more perishable. Store green onions wrapped in plastic in the refrigerator for about a week.

## preparation

There are many suggested methods for preventing tears while chopping onions, from wearing goggles to chopping under running water. Using a sharp knife so the onion cells are cut cleanly instead of being crushed helps. Sweet, red and green onions can be enjoyed raw. Yellow onions are more pungent, but become sweeter with long cooking.

## recipe suggestions

The mouthwatering smell of an onion sautéing is the start of so many delicious recipes. Slivers of raw red onion add a piquant touch to salads. For a stunning main course, whole baked onions can be stuffed with grain or vegetable mixtures. Green onions or sliced sweet onions are great on the grill.

# spinach fettuccine with garlic-onion sauce

½ cup (1 stick) dairy-free margarine
1 tablespoon olive oil
1 pound Vidalia or other sweet onions, sliced
12 cloves garlic, chopped
1 tablespoon agave syrup
¼ cup Marsala wine
Salt and black pepper
1 pound spinach fettuccine, cooked and drained according to package directions
Grated dairy-free Parmesan cheese alternative (optional)

1. Heat margarine and oil in large skillet over medium heat until margarine is melted. Add onions and garlic; cover and cook until soft. Add agave; reduce heat to low. Cook, uncovered, 30 minutes, stirring occasionally.

2. Add wine; cook 5 minutes. Season to taste with salt and pepper. Pour sauce over pasta; toss to coat. Sprinkle with cheese alternative; serve immediately. *Makes 4 servings*

## nutrients per serving:

| | |
|---|---|
| **Calories** 727 | **Total Fat** 28g |
| **Calories from Fat** 34% | **Saturated Fat** 10g |
| **Protein** 16g | **Cholesterol** 0mg |
| **Carbohydrate** 103g | **Sodium** 390mg |
| **Fiber** 6g | |

# Panko Bread Crumbs

Panko are the Japanese version of bread crumbs. They are flaky and light, crisper and crunchier than ordinary bread crumbs. Who would guess they could make such a difference?

## benefits

Panko means bread crumbs in Japanese. Compared to what we think of as "crumbs", panko are more like coarse flakes. Since they have a larger surface area, they form a lacy coating, which stays crisper longer and absorbs less grease when fried. Used in patties, stuffings or as a topping for casseroles, panko keeps textures lighter and less dense than regular bread crumbs.

## selection and storage

Panko was originally only available in Asian markets imported from Japan, but its popularity has made it much easier to find in ordinary supermarkets. Now several American companies produce panko and you can even choose panko flavored with herbs and spices. Do check ingredient lists carefully, however, as some panko is flavored with honey. Some brands also contain sugar, yeast and salt. There are now whole wheat panko bread crumbs available and even gluten-free versions. If your market doesn't carry panko, try purchasing it online. To keep panko crisp, store it in a sealed container in a cool, dry place.

## preparation

Unless you buy seasoned panko, the crumbs have virtually no flavor and are a blank canvas. You can add seasonings such as garlic powder, herbs, pepper and the like. Taste a bit before adding, since some panko does contain salt or sugar.

Toasting panko brings out the crispness and adds color. Spread it in a single layer in a baking pan and toast in a 425°F oven for 2 minutes or until lightly browned. Add even more flavor by toasting panko in a skillet with some olive oil.

## recipe suggestions

Anyplace you would use bread crumbs, panko may be substituted and the result will be lighter and crunchier. Panko is perfect for breading tofu as in the recipe here, or for making tempura. Try adding some seasoned or toasted panko to sautéed or roasted vegetables. Combine panko with finely chopped walnuts and nutritional yeast for a satisfying vegan version of Parmesan cheese to top pasta and other dishes.

# fried tofu with sesame dipping sauce

- 3 tablespoons soy sauce or tamari
- 2 tablespoons unseasoned rice wine vinegar
- 2 teaspoons sugar
- 1 teaspoon sesame seeds, toasted
- 1 teaspoon dark sesame oil
- ⅛ teaspoon red pepper flakes
- 1 package (14 ounces) extra firm tofu
- 2 tablespoons all-purpose flour
- ¼ cup rice milk or soymilk
- 1 tablespoon cornstarch
- ¾ cup panko bread crumbs
- 4 tablespoons vegetable oil

1. For dipping sauce, combine soy sauce, vinegar, sugar, sesame seeds, sesame oil and red pepper flakes in small bowl. Set aside.

2. Drain tofu and press between paper towels to remove excess water. Cut horizontally into four slices; cut each slice diagonally into triangles. Place flour in shallow dish. Stir rice milk into cornstarch in shallow bowl until smooth. Place panko in another shallow bowl.

3. Dip each piece of tofu in flour to lightly coat all sides; dip in rice milk mixture, turning to coat. Drain; roll in panko to coat lightly.

4. Heat 2 tablespoons vegetable oil in large nonstick skillet over high heat. Reduce heat to medium; add half of tofu in single layer. Cook 1 to 2 minutes per side or until golden brown. Repeat with remaining tofu and oil. Serve with dipping sauce.

*Makes 4 servings*

## nutrients per serving:

| | |
|---|---|
| **Calories** 659 | **Total Fat** 26g |
| **Calories from Fat** 35% | **Saturated Fat** 4g |
| **Protein** 13g | **Cholesterol** 0mg |
| **Carbohydrate** 58g | **Sodium** 1,585mg |
| **Fiber** 7g | |

# Parsnips

Pity the poor, pale parsnip. Its lumpy, frumpy appearance hides a complex sweetness and delicious starchiness that make potatoes seem a bit bland in comparison.

## benefits

In Europe parsnips were used as a sweetener before sugar was widely available. Because cold causes the parsnip to convert starches to sugar, they are even sweeter when harvested after the first frost, which makes them the ideal winter vegetable. Parsnips provide a good helping of fiber, as well as vitamin C, potassium, magnesium and folic acid. All that sweetness is also low in calories—only about 50 in a half a cup.

## selection and storage

Parsnips are in season in late fall and winter when they are at their best. Choose small to medium parsnips if possible. Large ones can be tough and often have a woody core that must be removed. In the produce section, parsnips are often stocked near and confused with parsley roots. One way to tell the difference is that parsley roots are sold with greens attached and parsnips aren't. This is because the leaves of parsnips produce a juice that can cause a rash on sensitive individuals. Pick parsnips that are sturdy and firm, not limp. The tops should have no sprouts and the color should be uniformly beige and smooth, without small roots poking out. Store unwashed parsnips in a loosely closed plastic bag in the crisper drawer of the refrigerator where they will last for at least several weeks depending on how old they were when purchased.

## preparation

Parsnips should be scrubbed well and peeled. Small, tender ones can be slivered or shredded and enjoyed raw in salads or slaws. Mature parsnips often have a woody core resembling the wick of a candle; remove it before or after cooking. Cut parsnips into pieces of the same size for even cooking.

## recipe suggestions

Roasted parsnips are delicious—cut them into chunks, toss with olive oil, salt and pepper and roast in a hot oven. Try mashing parsnips along with potatoes or winter squash to add subtle sweetness. Parsnips are also great in soups or stews. Add them during the last 10 to 15 minutes of cooking time so they don't become mushy.

## nutrients per serving:

| | | |
|---|---|---|
| **Calories** 296 | **Carbohydrate** 29g | **Saturated Fat** 6g |
| **Calories from Fat** 56% | **Fiber** 4g | **Cholesterol** 0mg |
| **Protein** 4g | **Total Fat** 19g | **Sodium** 182mg |

## parsnip patties

    1 pound parsnips, peeled and cut into
        ¾-inch chunks
    4 tablespoons (½ stick) dairy-free
        margarine, divided
    ¼ cup chopped onion
    ¼ cup all-purpose flour
    ⅓ cup dairy-free milk
    2 teaspoons chopped fresh chives
        Salt and black pepper
    ¾ cup fresh bread crumbs
    2 tablespoons vegetable oil

1. Pour 1 inch water into medium saucepan. Bring to a boil over high heat. Add parsnips; cover and cook 10 minutes or until fork-tender. Drain. Place in large bowl. Coarsely mash.

2. Melt 2 tablespoons margarine in small skillet over medium-high heat. Add onion; cook and stir until translucent. Whisk in flour until bubbly and lightly browned. Whisk in dairy-free milk until thickened. Stir flour mixture into mashed parsnips. Stir in chives; season with salt and pepper.

3. Form parsnip mixture into four patties. Spread bread crumbs on plate. Dip patties in bread crumbs to coat all sides evenly. Place on waxed paper and refrigerate 2 hours.

4. Heat remaining 2 tablespoons margarine and oil in large skillet over medium-high heat until margarine is melted and bubbly. Add patties; cook 5 minutes per side or until browned.                    *Makes 4 servings*

# Pasta

What could be simpler than pasta? It's nothing more than flour and water. But this simplicity comes in hundreds of shapes and sizes with millions of delicious ways to enjoy it.

## benefits

Pasta just may be the ultimate convenience food, especially for vegans and vegetarians. It's a pantry staple that's quick to prepare and turns any vegetable into a healthy, satisfying meal. Pasta provides complex carbohydrates for sustained energy plus the B vitamins the body needs to help turn those carbs into fuel. Whole wheat or multigrain pasta adds more fiber, plus a heartier flavor.

## selection and storage

Depending on who's doing the counting, estimates claim that there are at least 600 different pasta shapes. Dried pastas are almost always vegan. Fresh pastas, found in the refrigerated case, often contain eggs. The best dried pasta is made from 100% semolina flour, ground from high-protein durum wheat. It creates noodles that cook up firm and al dente. Good pasta should have a bright amber color and a matte finish. Dried pasta can be stored in a tightly closed package in a cupboard for several years.

## preparation

Bringing a big pot of water to a boil to cook pasta takes time, so don't leave it to the last minute. Salting the water is not required, but can be important for flavor. How much salt? There are as many answers to that question as there are Italian grandmas. For 6 quarts of water you'll need at least a few tablespoons. Add the pasta only after the water is at a full boil. Stir gently to keep the noodles from sticking together. Check package directions for timing, but the best way to know pasta is al dente and done to your liking is to remove a piece and taste it. Remember that residual heat will continue cooking the pasta while it drains. It's better to err on the side of slightly undercooked.

## recipe suggestions

There is no more versatile ingredient than pasta. It can be matched with just about any ingredient you have on hand, from canned beans to fresh herbs. Try a sauce made from pumpkin, escarole or fennel for a change of pace.

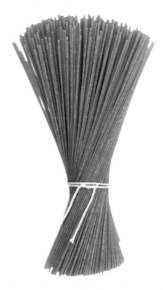

# whole wheat penne pasta with summer vegetables

- **6 ounces uncooked whole wheat penne pasta (about 2 cups)**
- **2 teaspoons olive oil**
- **1½ cups chopped fresh broccoli**
- **1 medium zucchini, chopped**
- **½ medium yellow bell pepper, chopped**
- **2 cloves garlic, minced**
- **8 ounces (about 1½ cups) cherry or grape tomatoes, halved**
- **1 cup mushrooms, sliced**
- **½ teaspoon dried oregano**
- **¾ cup crumbled dairy-free feta cheese\***

*\*Use purchased dairy-free feta or prepare dairy-free feta (page 65).*

**1.** Cook pasta according to package directions. Drain and keep warm.

**2.** Heat oil in large nonstick skillet over medium-high heat. Add broccoli, zucchini, bell pepper and garlic. Cook and stir about 2 minutes or until vegetables begin to soften.

**3.** Stir in tomatoes, mushrooms and oregano. Reduce heat to medium and cook and stir about 8 minutes or until vegetables are tender and tomatoes release their juices.

**4.** Stir vegetables into pasta. Add dairy-free feta; toss to mix well. *Makes 4 servings*

## nutrients per serving:

**Calories** 257
**Calories from Fat** 19%
**Protein** 10g
**Carbohydrate** 45g
**Fiber** 6g
**Total Fat** 6g
**Saturated Fat** 1g
**Cholesterol** 0mg
**Sodium** 239mg

# Peanuts

Please pass the peanuts! From a PB&J sandwich to a sack of peanuts at the ball game, this all-American nut, which is actually a legume, has a place in our cuisine and our hearts.

## benefits

Peanuts and peanut butter have often been considered guilt-inducing, high-fat foods. The truth is that their fat is mostly the heart-healthy monounsaturated kind. Peanuts are also a great source of protein and fiber. They even contain resveratrol, the beneficial antioxidant in red wine that seems to be linked to lowering the risk of inflammation and blood clotting. It may be the peanut's incredible versatility that is the most important benefit. Peanuts can star in savory main courses, sweet desserts, sauces, soups and so much more.

## selection and storage

Peanuts in their shells are sold roasted with or without salt. To judge freshness, pick up a peanut and shake it. It should not rattle as that is a sign the kernels have dried out. Shells should be free from cracks or dark spots. Shelled peanuts are available oil- or dry-roasted in vacuum-sealed containers or bulk bins. Check for any sign of insect or moisture damage. If possible take a sniff to make sure they do not smell musty or rancid. At home, shelled peanuts should be stored in a tightly sealed container in the refrigerator for up to three months or in the freezer up to six months. Peanut butter in its purest form is just ground peanuts. Be aware that many commercial brands contain sugar and other additives. After opening, store natural peanut butter in the refrigerator for up to six months.

## preparation

Making peanut butter yourself is easy if you have a food processor. Process the nuts with enough vegetable oil to make a smooth paste and season with salt.

## recipe suggestions

Sprinkle chopped peanuts on salads or vegetable dishes for a crunchy garnish. Add some peanut butter to your morning smoothie for a protein boost. Asian and African cuisines have many savory soups, stews and sauces that use peanuts or peanut butter. (See the recipe on the next page.) Peanut butter pairs beautifully with apples, pears, bananas, carrots or celery for a healthy snack.

132

# asian noodles with peanut sauce

- ½ package (about 4 ounces) uncooked udon noodles
- 1 tablespoon vegetable oil
- 2 cups snow peas, cut diagonally into bite-size pieces
- 1 cup shredded carrots
- ¼ cup chopped green onions
- ¼ cup hot water
- ¼ cup peanut butter
- 2 to 4 tablespoons hot chili sauce with garlic
- 1 tablespoon soy sauce
- ¼ cup dry-roasted peanuts
- Sliced red jalapeño (optional)

1. Cook noodles according to package directions. Drain.

2. Heat oil in large skillet over medium-high heat. Add snow peas and carrots; stir-fry 2 minutes. Remove from heat.

3. Add green onions, water, peanut butter, chili sauce and soy sauce to skillet; mix well. Stir in noodles; toss to coat. Sprinkle with peanuts and garnish with jalapeño.

*Makes 4 servings*

## nutrients per serving:

**Calories** 323
**Calories from Fat 47**%
**Protein** 12g
**Carbohydrate** 33g
**Fiber** 5g
**Total Fat** 17g
**Saturated Fat** 3g
**Cholesterol** 0mg
**Sodium** 756mg

# Phyllo Dough

Phyllo is phenomenal. You can turn this paper-thin wheat flour dough into appetizers, desserts and wraps of all kinds. It can be layered, folded, rolled, ruffled or used as a crust.

## benefits

Stretching raw dough into incredibly thin sheets of phyllo is a time-consuming skill and an art developed by the Greeks centuries ago. Fortunately we can purchase ready-made phyllo and it is almost always vegan. (Most of the Greek pastries made from phyllo are not vegan since butter is often used between the layers or the filling contains feta cheese.) A little phyllo goes a long way. While it doesn't contribute much nutrition (it's mostly flour and water) five sheets of regular phyllo have only 160 calories.

## selection and storage

Phyllo (sometimes spelled fillo) most often comes in rectangular boxes stocked in the freezer section near pastries and pie crust. Each package usually contains one pound of phyllo, which will be between 20 and 40 sheets, depending on thickness. Sheets are generally 9 by 14 inches or 14 by 18 inches. You can also purchase preshaped phyllo cups and shredded phyllo dough, which is called kataifi. Check sell-by dates and remember that phyllo must be thawed completely before using it.

## preparation

While it has a reputation for being difficult to work with, phyllo is very forgiving as long as you remember one important rule: It dries out in a heartbeat, so keep phyllo covered. Do not even open the box until you have all the other ingredients assembled and you are ready to work. Keep all phyllo, other than the piece you are currently working on, covered with plastic wrap and a damp towel. If you are stacking phyllo, spray with cooking spray or brush gently with oil between layers. If the phyllo tears, don't panic. You can patch it with another sheet. To prevent leaking, fillings should be chilled and not too moist.

## recipe suggestions

Phyllo is a good vegan replacement for puff pastry, which usually contains butter. Try it as a crust for a tart or pizza or use it as a topper for a casserole. Wrap cooked vegetables in phyllo for elegant main courses or appetizers.

# almond-pear strudel

- 5 to 6 cups thinly sliced crisp pears (4 to 5 medium pears)
- 1 tablespoon grated lemon peel
- 1 tablespoon lemon juice
- 6 sheets (¼ pound) phyllo dough
- ¼ cup (½ stick) dairy-free margarine, melted
- ⅓ cup plus 1 teaspoon sugar, divided
- 2 teaspoons ground cinnamon
- 1 teaspoon ground nutmeg
- ½ teaspoon almond extract
- ¾ cup slivered almonds, toasted, divided

1. Preheat oven to 400°F. Spray baking sheet with nonstick cooking spray.

2. Combine pears, lemon peel and lemon juice in large microwavable bowl. Microwave on HIGH 6 minutes or until tender; set aside.

3. Cover work surface with plastic wrap. Place one phyllo sheet on plastic wrap. (Cover remaining phyllo with damp kitchen towel to prevent drying out.) Brush 1 teaspoon margarine over phyllo sheet. Top with second phyllo sheet; brush with 1 teaspoon margarine. Repeat layers with remaining phyllo and 5 teaspoons margarine.

4. Combine ⅓ cup sugar, cinnamon and nutmeg in medium bowl. Drain pears and toss with sugar mixture and almond extract.

5. Spread pear mixture evenly over phyllo, leaving 3-inch strip on far long side. Sprinkle pears with ½ cup almonds. Brush strip with 2 teaspoons margarine. Beginning at long side of phyllo closest to you, carefully roll up jelly-roll style, using plastic wrap to gently lift. Place strudel, seam side down, on prepared baking sheet. Brush top with 1 teaspoon margarine.

6. Bake 20 minutes or until golden. Brush with remaining margarine. Sprinkle with remaining ¼ cup almonds and 1 teaspoon sugar. Bake 5 minutes. Cool 10 minutes before serving. *Makes 8 servings*

## nutrients per serving:

**Calories** 250
**Calories from Fat** 40%
**Protein** 4g
**Carbohydrate** 35g
**Fiber** 5g
**Total Fat** 12g
**Saturated Fat** 3g
**Cholesterol** 0mg
**Sodium** 130mg

# Pineapple

Pineapple brings us the sunny taste of the tropics. Both sweet and tart, pineapple brightens anything from a morning smoothie to dessert on a dreary winter evening.

## benefits

Pineapples are native to the Americas and can only be grown in the tropics. Since they were difficult to ship in colonial times, pineapples were considered a rare treat suitable for honored guests. The pineapple shape is still a symbol of hospitality, but now we can buy a pineapple at any supermarket. Pineapples are a very good source of vitamin C and they contain an enzyme called bromelain, which appears to be a useful anti-inflammatory as well as an aid to digestion.

## selection and storage

To find the best pineapple let your nose be your guide. Pineapples begin to ripen from the bottom, so take a sniff. It should smell sweet and fresh. If the smell is slightly fermented and sickly sweet, the fruit is deteriorating. The pineapple should be golden yellow at least at its base. A completely green pineapple will never ripen. Yellow leaves, dark sunken eyes or soft spots are all signs that the pineapple is past its prime. Store pineapple for two days at room temperature or up to five days refrigerated. Once cut, refrigerate pineapple pieces covered in juice in an airtight container for up to five days. Pineapple is also available canned in slices, chunks or crushed, packed in juice or sugar syrup.

## preparation

Many supermarkets have special machines that will slice and core a fresh pineapple. To do it yourself, place the pineapple on a cutting board with a trough to catch the juice. Cut off the tough skin with a sharp knife in a downward motion following the curve of the fruit. Remove any woody "eyes" you missed with the tip of a paring knife. You can squeeze the skins to produce more sweet pineapple juice.

## recipe suggestions

Perfectly ripe fresh pineapple is dessert all by itself. Spiff it up with a splash of rum and some toasted coconut for fancier fare. It's also excellent grilled in slices or on veggie kabobs. Pineapple works well in a fruit salad and belongs in sweet and sour dishes.

# gingered pineapple and cranberries

- 2 cans (20 ounces each) pineapple chunks in juice, undrained
- 1 cup dried sweetened cranberries
- ½ cup packed brown sugar
- 1 teaspoon curry powder, divided
- 1 teaspoon grated fresh ginger, divided
- ¼ teaspoon red pepper flakes
- 2 tablespoons water
- 1 tablespoon cornstarch

**Slow Cooker Directions**

1. Place pineapple with juice, cranberries, brown sugar, ½ teaspoon curry powder, ½ teaspoon ginger and pepper flakes in 1½-quart slow cooker. Cover; cook on HIGH 3 hours.

2. Combine water, cornstarch, remaining ½ teaspoon curry powder and ½ teaspoon ginger in small bowl; stir until cornstarch is dissolved. Add to pineapple mixture. Cook, uncovered, on HIGH 15 minutes or until thickened. *Makes 4½ cups*

**Variation:** Substitute 2 cans (20 ounces each) pineapple tidbits in heavy syrup for pineapple and brown sugar.

## nutrients per serving:

**Calories** 84
**Calories from Fat** 2%
**Protein** <1g
**Carbohydrate** 22g
**Fiber** 1g

**Total Fat** <1g
**Saturated Fat** 0g
**Cholesterol** 0mg
**Sodium** 3mg

# Potatoes

Pick the potatoes that please your palate—cute fingerlings, purple potatoes, heirloom varieties no bigger than a marble, or giant russet bakers.

## benefits

Potatoes have gotten a bad rap for being high-carb, starchy calories. It's not deserved. Potatoes are a very good source of vitamin C, vitamin B₆ and potassium and also offer a variety of phytochemicals. (Of course if you eat them as greasy French fries or chips, that's another story.) Potatoes are economical, even if you're purchasing specialty varieties, easy to prepare and supremely satisfying. In a plant-based diet their versatility is especially welcome. They pair with just about anything and will obligingly go from soft and fluffy to crisp and browned based on how they are cooked.

## selection and storage

There are hundreds of varieties of potatoes in many shapes and sizes. The familiar brown-skinned russet is the standard for baking or mashing because of its fluffy, starchy interior. Red potatoes keep their shape better after cooking so are perfect for potato salads or gratins. White and golden potatoes usually have a dense creamy flesh and thin skins so are good for mashing, skins and all. Fingerlings come in a range of colors and have a firm, waxy texture. They are delicious steamed, pan-fried or grilled. New potatoes are simply those that have just been dug and can be any variety. Choose potatoes that are firm and smooth without wrinkling, green spots or sprouts. Potatoes should be stored in a well-ventilated place that is cool and dark. Keep them away from onions— a chemical reaction can speed spoilage of both. Do not store them in the refrigerator where they will become sweet. Mature potatoes will keep up to two weeks; new potatoes last only about a week.

## preparation

Just before cooking, scrub potatoes well with a vegetable brush. Cut away sprouts or bad spots. A greenish tinge means a potato has been exposed to light and has produced solanine, which is poisonous in large quantities. Cut away and discard any green areas before cooking.

## recipe suggestions

Potatoes take well to any cooking method. Use the microwave as a timesaving jump start for potatoes you will sauté or grill. Bake extra potatoes and use the leftovers for hash browns later.

# monterey potato hash

- 2 tablespoons olive oil
- 4 small baking potatoes, cut into ¼-inch slices
- 1 medium red onion, sliced
- 2 cloves garlic, minced
- 1 teaspoon dried basil or oregano
- ¼ teaspoon salt
- ¼ teaspoon black pepper
- 1 cup water
- 1 large green bell pepper, halved and cut into ¼-inch slices
- 1 cup cherry tomatoes, cut into halves
- ¼ cup (1 ounce) shredded dairy-free cheese alternative

1. Heat wok or large skillet over high heat about 1 minute. Drizzle oil into wok and heat 30 seconds. Add potatoes; cook about 8 minutes or until lightly browned, stirring often. Reduce heat to medium. Add onion, garlic, basil, salt and black pepper; stir-fry 1 minute.

2. Stir in water; cover and cook 5 minutes or until potatoes are fork-tender, gently stirring once. Add bell pepper; stir-fry until water evaporates. Gently stir in tomatoes; cook until heated through. Sprinkle with dairy-free cheese.          *Makes 4 to 6 servings*

## nutrients per serving:

| | |
|---|---|
| **Calories** 266 | **Cholesterol** 0mg |
| **Calories from Fat** 27% | **Sodium** 261mg |
| **Protein** 7g | |
| **Carbohydrate** 43g | |
| **Fiber** 5g | |
| **Total Fat** 8g | |
| **Saturated Fat** 1g | |

# Quinoa

Quinoa is called a super grain since it's a complete protein that's also rich in fiber and iron. Oh, yes, it also has a nutty, sweet taste and cooks in 15 minutes!

## benefits

If you're only going to add one new grain to your cooking repertoire, make it quinoa (pronounced "KEEN-wah"). The Incas considered it sacred and called it the mother of all grains. Quinoa is the only grain that is a complete protein, meaning it provides all of the essential amino acids. It's also gluten-free and an excellent source of minerals, including iron, magnesium potassium, phosphorus and zinc. There are more nutritional benefits, but maybe the best benefit is that quinoa is quick and easy to prepare and easy to digest.

## selection and storage

Quinoa is now readily available packaged in most supermarkets as well as in bulk bins. Purchase it in a store that is likely to have high turnover, like a natural foods store. Varieties range in color from pale ivory to almost black, but the most commonly available are regular or white quinoa and red quinoa. They have similar amounts of protein, but white quinoa is slightly lower in calories and has more fiber. Red quinoa is slightly chewier and crunchier than white when cooked. Store quinoa in a sealed container away from heat and moisture.

## preparation

Quinoa is naturally coated with a bitter substance called saponin, which protects it from insects when it's growing. The grain is rinsed during processing to remove the saponin, but it doesn't hurt to rinse it again before cooking. Place quinoa in a fine-mesh strainer and swish the grains around under cold running water. If the water looks cloudy or soapy that's the saponin. To cook regular quinoa, use one part quinoa to two parts water or broth. Bring to a simmer, then reduce heat to low. Cover and simmer 15 minutes or until quinoa is tender and water is absorbed. Let it sit, covered, 5 minutes, then fluff with a fork.

## recipe suggestions

Try quinoa as a change from rice, potatoes or pasta. Quinoa can be a substitute for bulgur wheat in tabbouleh. It is also an excellent breakfast porridge.

# Radishes

There is a world of radishes beyond the familiar red globes we enjoy raw. Asian radishes come in many colors and can be braised, roasted, pickled or added to soups.

## benefits

Radishes are members of the cruciferous family (like cabbage) and contain similar cancer-protective properties. They are high in fiber and vitamin C and very low in calories. Their pretty red color adds a crisp spicy bite to salads, hors d'oeuvres and crudités platters. Don't forget the fresh radish greens either. They can be sautéed for an even bigger nutritional boost.

## selection and storage

Spring radishes are the most common in our markets. In season,

especially at farmers' markets, you will find examples not only of the familiar Red Globe but also multi-colored Easter Egg radishes and French Breakfast radishes that are elongated and white at their tips. Icicle radishes are white and tapered as their name suggests. If possible purchase radishes with the greens attached. Not only are the greens edible, they are a sign the radish is fresh. The root itself should be firm and free of cracks. Spiciness varies depending on many things, from where it was grown to how mature it is. Even two radishes from the same bunch may have different levels of heat.

The best known Asian radish is the daikon, a smooth, white, tapered radish that is usually 10 to 20 inches long and can weigh several pounds. Choose very firm roots, preferably with greens attached. Smaller is not

necessarily better. All radishes should have their leaves removed before being stored. They will keep for about a week in the refrigerator.

## preparation

Radishes need to be well scrubbed, but not peeled. The greens need to be washed in several changes of water as they tend to be muddy and sandy. Slice off the root end of the radish and trim the top where the greens were attached.

## recipe suggestions

Sliced radishes, especially large daikons, make great bases for canapés of all kinds. Sweet spring radishes, thinly sliced, are delightful in open-face sandwiches on dark bread. Sautéed or roasted, radishes become sweeter and more turniplike. Sliced or diced daikons are often added to Asian soup and noodle dishes.

# Seitan

It sounds mysterious, but seitan, also called wheat-meat or mock duck, has been a favorite of Asian vegetarians since the seventh century. It's made from the gluten in flour and mimics many kinds of meat.

## benefits

Seitan (pronounced "SAY-tan") is made from wheat that has had the starch washed away until only the wheat protein (gluten) remains. If you've eaten mock chicken, beef or pork in a Chinese restaurant, you've probably tried seitan. It is also the base for some commercial vegetarian deli "meats." The chewy consistency of seitan is very close to meat and like tofu and tempeh it will take on the flavor of whatever you marinate or cook with it. It is a good choice as a meat alternative for those who are trying to cut down on soy products.

## selection and storage

Seitan can be purchased in the refrigerated section of natural food stores and Asian markets in many forms and flavors. It comes water-packed like tofu or vacuum-sealed and flavored Asian style with soy or as imitation chicken or beef. In Asian markets you will also find flavored seitan in cans, which are labeled mock duck or chicken.

It is not difficult to make your own seitan at home. You will need to start from a product called vital wheat gluten, which is wheat flour that has already had the starch removed. The process involves kneading liquid and seasonings into the vital wheat gluten and then simmering it in a flavored broth. You can also purchase seitan-making kits. Instructions and kits are readily available online.

## preparation

Seitan is sold in blocks, strips or chunks, and much of it is flavored, so choose a product based on your recipe. Water-packed seitan should be drained thoroughly and can be rinsed to reduce sodium. The sodium content of prepared seitan tends to be high, so be judicious when adding soy sauce or salt in cooking.

## recipe suggestions

Seitan will obligingly imitate just about any form of meat. You can use chunks or strips in stir-fries, fajitas and stews in place of the meat called for in the original recipes. Because it readily absorbs flavor, seitan is also great on the grill brushed with barbecue sauce.

# thai seitan stir-fry

- 1 package (8 ounces) seitan, drained and thinly sliced
- 1 jalapeño pepper, halved and seeded
- 3 cloves garlic
- 1 piece (1 inch) peeled fresh ginger
- ⅓ cup soy sauce
- ¼ cup packed brown sugar
- ¼ cup lime juice
- ½ teaspoon red pepper flakes
- ¼ teaspoon salt
- 3 tablespoons vegetable oil
- 1 medium onion, chopped
- 2 red bell peppers, thinly sliced
- 2 cups broccoli florets
- 4 cups lightly packed baby spinach
- ¼ cup shredded fresh basil
- 3 cups hot cooked rice
- 3 green onions, sliced diagonally
- ¼ cup peanuts, chopped

1. Place seitan in medium bowl. Combine jalapeño, garlic and ginger in food processor; process until finely chopped. Add soy sauce, brown sugar, lime juice, red pepper flakes and salt; process until blended. Pour mixture over seitan; stir to coat. Marinate at least 20 minutes at room temperature.

2. Heat oil in wok or large skillet over high heat. Add onion, bell peppers and broccoli; stir-fry 3 to 5 minutes. Add seitan, marinade and green onions. Bring to a boil; stir-fry 3 minutes or until vegetables are crisp-tender and seitan is hot. Add spinach in two additions, stirring until beginning to wilt after each addition.

3. Stir in basil just before serving. Serve over rice; sprinkle with green onions and peanuts.

*Makes 4 to 6 servings*

## nutrients per serving:

| | |
|---|---|
| **Calories** 489 | **Total Fat** 16g |
| **Calories from Fat** 29% | **Saturated Fat** 2g |
| **Protein** 22g | **Cholesterol** 0mg |
| **Carbohydrate** 67g | **Sodium** 2,314mg |
| **Fiber** 6g | |

# Sesame Oil

Before 600 BC sesame oil was used as a food, a salve and a medication. As a cooking oil or condiment, sesame oil provides unique flavor, aroma and health benefits.

## benefits

Sesame seeds were one of the first crops processed for oil and sesame oil figures prominently in Indian ayurvedic medicine as well as in many holistic healing regimens. Most of the fat in sesame oil is polyunsaturated or monounsaturated and so is considered heart-healthy. In cooking, toasted or dark sesame oil is essential for the characteristic flavor of many Asian dishes. Light sesame oil has a milder, nutty flavor and is better for frying.

## selection and storage

Dark and light sesame oil are not interchangeable as they have very different flavors. Dark sesame oil comes from toasted seeds. It is most often used as a flavoring element added towards the end of cooking time. It is quite perishable and once opened should be refrigerated for no longer than a year. Refined light sesame oil is best for high heat applications and is used much less often. Check labels when purchasing sesame oil to make sure you are getting pure sesame oil and not one diluted with other oils, which are less expensive. All oils are perishable and are damaged by heat and light. If any oil smells off, it's becoming rancid and should be discarded. You can extend shelf life by storing oils in the refrigerator. Don't be concerned if the oil becomes cloudy or solidifies. It will return to normal at room temperature and this will not affect flavor.

## preparation

Dark sesame oil has an intense flavor and a little goes a long way. Many recipes will call for mixing a small amount of sesame oil with other flavorings to make a marinade or sauce. If you are concerned that the sesame oil will overpower other flavors, use less. You can always add a bit more at the end of cooking time.

## recipe suggestions

Dark sesame oil is delicious drizzled over roasted vegetables of all kinds. It pairs well with soy sauce in dips for pot stickers or in a marinade for tofu and is used in peanut sauces for noodle dishes.

# rich roasted sesame vegetables

1 carrot, peeled and cut into 2-inch pieces
4 ounces sweet potato, peeled and cut
    into ¾-inch cubes
½ red bell pepper, cut into 1-inch cubes
½ medium onion, cut into ½-inch wedges
1 tablespoon sesame oil, divided
2 teaspoons sugar, divided
¼ teaspoon salt

1. Preheat oven to 425°F. Line baking sheet with foil. Place carrot, potato, bell pepper and onion on baking sheet. Sprinkle evenly with 2 teaspoons oil, 1 teaspoon sugar and salt. Stir gently to coat; spread in single layer.

2. Bake 20 minutes or until edges are browned and potatoes are fork-tender, stirring once halfway through.

3. Sprinkle vegetables with remaining 1 teaspoon oil and 1 teaspoon sugar. Toss gently to coat.            *Makes 2 servings*

**Serving Suggestion:** Sprinkle vegetables with a little rice wine vinegar or lime juice before serving.

# Sesame Seeds

Open sesame! Ground into tahini or sprinkled on breadsticks, these tiny seeds open up a whole world of flavors and textures wherever they go.

## benefits

Sesame seeds not only add a delicate crunch and nutty taste to foods, they also boost nutrients. They are rich in many minerals, including copper, magnesium and calcium. Plus, sesame seeds contain phytonutrients called lignans that have been shown to fight certain hormone-related cancers, including those of the breast and prostate. Tahini, the paste made from ground sesame seeds, is a necessary ingredient in hummus and can be used instead of butter or peanut butter as a spread for sandwiches.

## selection and storage

Sesame seeds come in different colors, depending on the variety, including brown, red, black and yellow, but the most common is a pale ivory. They can be purchased hulled or unhulled. The hull is a thin edible outer shell that is often removed since it has a slightly bitter flavor. You can purchase sesame seeds in the spice section at supermarkets, but Middle Eastern markets may have a better selection and lower prices. The seeds are quite perishable, so buy them someplace that has a high turnover and in small quantities that you will use quickly. Store them in an airtight container in a cool, dry place. Better yet, refrigerate or freeze them. They will keep about six months in the refrigerator and up to a year in the freezer. Tahini can be found in jars or tubs near the nut butters.

## preparation

To toast sesame seeds spread them in a single layer on a rimmed baking sheet. Bake in a 350°F oven 5 minutes or until fragrant, stirring once or twice. Immediately transfer to a bowl to prevent burning.

## recipe suggestions

For a versatile tahini sauce, whisk together 1/2 cup of tahini, 1/4 cup of lemon juice, 1/4 cup of olive oil, plus minced garlic, cumin, salt and pepper. Add water to thin to desired consistency and serve with falafel or steamed vegetables. Toasted sesame seeds add crunch to salads and cereals. Black sesame seeds make a pretty garnish for rice and vegetable dishes.

# vegetable-topped hummus

- 1 can (about 15 ounces) chickpeas, rinsed and drained
- 2 tablespoons tahini
- 2 tablespoons lemon juice
- 1 clove garlic
- ¾ teaspoon salt
- 1 tomato, finely chopped
- 2 green onions, finely chopped
- 2 tablespoons chopped fresh parsley
  Pita bread or cut-up vegetables (optional)

1. Combine chickpeas, tahini, lemon juice, garlic and salt in food processor or blender; process until smooth.

2. Combine tomato, onions and parsley in small bowl.

3. Place hummus in medium bowl; top with tomato mixture. Serve with pita bread or vegetables, if desired.     *Makes 8 servings*

# Shallots

Dainty, coppery-pink shallots are like onions with a French accent. They look a bit like garlic, another relative, but have a flavor that is milder and more complex than either one.

## benefits

Shallots are part of the Allium family, which includes onions and garlic, but shallots actually have more vitamin A, protein, calcium and iron than the same amount of onions. Because they are milder, shallots are also a bit less likely to make you cry. Their tenderness makes them a better choice for raw use and they are often added to vinaigrettes and uncooked sauces for this reason. Shallots are easier to digest than garlic or onions and won't give you bad breath.

## selection and storage

Like garlic, shallots grow in clusters that are attached at the root end. Once cleaned and graded the bulbs are often separated. Some varieties are long and tapered, others nearly round. They should be of a size that there are between 10 and 20 in a pound. Larger specimens are most likely long onions, sometimes called torpedo shallots and don't offer quite the same flavor. Choose shallots that are firm and heavy for their size without soft spots. They should have dry, crackling skins and no dustiness or mold. Sprouting shallots are past their prime. Store shallots like onions in a dry, dark place with plenty of air circulation. They should last for several weeks.

## preparation

Skins can be loosened by covering shallots with boiling water for five minutes. To peel, cut off the tip and pull off the thin skin with a knife working towards the root end. Try not to peel off a layer of flesh with the skin.

Shallots may be substituted for onions for a gentler, different flavor: use three or four shallots to replace one onion.

## recipe suggestions

Add raw minced shallots to vinaigrettes and other salad dressings. They are a traditional foundation for French sauces, especially those made with wine. In Southeast Asian cuisine, shallots are an important part of curry pastes and are also fried for a crunchy garnish on noodle and rice dishes. Whole shallots can be roasted, braised or sautéed by themselves or with other vegetables.

## fusilli pizzaiolo

1 package (16 ounces) uncooked fusilli
    pasta
¼ cup olive oil
8 ounces mushrooms, sliced
1 large red bell pepper, chopped
1 large green bell pepper, chopped
1 large yellow bell pepper, chopped
5 large shallots, chopped
5 green onions, chopped
1 large onion, diced
8 cloves garlic, coarsely chopped
½ cup chopped fresh basil
2 tablespoons chopped fresh oregano
    Dash red pepper flakes
1 can (28 ounces) whole plum tomatoes,
    undrained and chopped
    Salt and black pepper

1. Cook fusilli according to package directions. Drain and keep warm.

2. Heat oil in large skillet over medium-high heat. Cook and stir mushrooms, bell peppers, shallots, onions, garlic, basil, oregano and red pepper flakes until lightly browned.

3. Add tomatoes with juice; bring to a boil. Reduce heat to low; simmer, uncovered, 20 minutes. Season with salt and black pepper. Toss pasta with sauce.

*Makes 6 to 8 servings*

### nutrients per serving:

**Calories** 444
**Calories from Fat** 21%
**Protein** 14g
**Carbohydrate** 75g
**Fiber** 7g
**Total Fat** 11g

**Saturated Fat** 2g
**Cholesterol** 0mg
**Sodium** 242mg

# Shiitake Mushrooms

Simple shiitakes can elevate vegetable or grain dishes to gourmet status. Their complex flavor blends a touch of smoke with a hint of pine and autumn leaves.

## benefits

Shiitakes are such a popular mushroom in Japan that they are used to flavor drinks, cookies and candies! No need to go that far, but it is one indication that this mushroom stands out in terms of flavor. Shiitakes stand out in other ways, too. They are a symbol of longevity in Asia and have been used in Chinese medicine for thousands of years. They appear to have antiviral and immunity boosting properties. Shiitakes are also a good source of riboflavin, niacin and vitamin $B_6$, which are important for the vegan diet, and they add texture and protein to vegan dishes.

## selection and storage

Fresh shiitakes have become plentiful and affordable thanks to the fact that they can be cultivated. Dried shiitakes are sometimes called Chinese black mushrooms and have a concentrated, more intense flavor. (See page 74 for more information.) Choose fresh shiitakes that have solid, thick caps, not those that are very thin or curled up. The mushrooms should be dry, but not leathery and should smell fresh. Avoid any without stems or those that have cracked stems. Never store mushrooms in plastic, which causes them to spoil quickly and become slimy. Instead, refrigerate them in a brown (unwaxed) paper bag. Shiitakes will keep for up to a week, but the sooner you use them, the better the flavor.

## preparation

Wipe shiitake caps with a damp cloth or rinse them off gingerly in cold running water. You don't want water to penetrate the mushroom and make it soggy. Cut off the tough stems, which can be used to flavor stocks. Shiitakes can be cooked any way you would other mushrooms, but be aware that they are drier and can burn more easily.

## recipe suggestions

Shiitakes' rich savoriness works extremely well with hearty grains like brown rice, barley, kamut or whole wheat. Shiitakes make an excellent base for a soup or broth. Roasting or grilling brings out their meaty texture and concentrates their flavor.

# soba stir-fry

8 ounces uncooked soba (buckwheat) noodles
1 tablespoon olive oil
2 cups sliced shiitake mushrooms
1 medium red bell pepper, cut into thin strips
2 whole dried red chiles *or* ¼ teaspoon red pepper flakes
1 clove garlic, minced
2 cups shredded napa cabbage
½ cup reduced-sodium vegetable broth
2 tablespoons reduced-sodium tamari or soy sauce
1 tablespoon rice wine or dry sherry
2 teaspoons cornstarch
1 package (14 ounces) firm tofu, drained and cut into 1-inch cubes
2 green onions, thinly sliced

1. Cook noodles according to package directions. Drain and set aside.

2. Heat oil in large nonstick skillet or wok over medium heat. Add mushrooms, bell pepper, dried chiles and garlic. Cook and stir 3 minutes or until mushrooms are tender. Add cabbage. Cover; cook 2 minutes or until cabbage is wilted.

3. Combine broth, tamari, rice wine and cornstarch in small bowl. Stir sauce into vegetable mixture. Cook 2 minutes or until sauce is thickened.

4. Stir in tofu and noodles; toss gently until heated through. Sprinkle with green onions. Remove and discard chiles. Serve immediately.          *Makes 4 (2-cup) servings*

## nutrients per serving:

| | |
|---|---|
| **Calories** 443 | **Total Fat** 13g |
| **Calories from Fat** 24% | **Saturated Fat** 2g |
| **Protein** 27g | **Cholesterol** 0mg |
| **Carbohydrate** 64g | **Sodium** 773mg |
| **Fiber** 6g | |

# Soy Sauce

Think of Asian cuisine and the first ingredient that comes to mind is soy sauce, but there's a lot more to it than the bottle on the table at the Chinese restaurant.

## benefits

Soy sauce and Japanese tamari, which is similar, have sometimes been labeled unhealthy since they are high in sodium. But if you use soy sauce instead of salt in your cooking, you'll get considerably more flavor for the same amount of sodium. Instead of sprinkling your food with a mineral, you'll be enjoying a condiment made by a natural process that has been enjoyed for thousands of years. (If you have medical reasons to watch your salt intake, you may want to limit your use of soy sauce or opt for a low-sodium version.) Soy sauce is made by brewing soybeans with roasted wheat or barley. Tamari is usually a bit thicker and is derived from miso. Tamari usually does not contain grain as an ingredient, which is important for those who are gluten sensitive.

## selection and storage

Visit an Asian grocery store and you'll find a staggering array of soy sauce, including dark, thin, light, mushroom-flavored and many more. There are really three basic types you need to know. What we consider regular soy sauce is Chinese light or thin soy. Check labels and be sure you are buying a brewed product. Cheaper sauces are manufactured from hydrolyzed vegetable protein with corn syrup and color added. Some Chinese dishes call for light and dark (sometimes called sweet or thick) soy sauces in the same recipe. Dark soy is brewed longer, is thicker and has molasses or caramel added. It has a richer, more full-bodied flavor. Tamari is Japanese soy sauce. Look for traditionally brewed brands. Once opened, store soy sauce in the refrigerator to preserve flavor longer. It should keep for up to a year.

## preparation

Soy sauce is most often mixed with other ingredients in a marinade or sauce. Because it is salty, be careful with long cooking methods that can concentrate flavors and always taste before adding salt.

## recipe suggestions

Soy sauce is an excellent ingredient in marinades for grill recipes of all kinds. Use it for an Asian-inspired salad dressing along with rice wine vinegar, ginger, garlic and honey.

# tofu satay with peanut sauce

## Satay

- 1 package (14 ounces) firm tofu, drained and pressed
- ⅓ cup water
- ⅓ cup soy sauce
- 1 tablespoon sesame oil
- 1 teaspoon minced garlic
- 1 teaspoon minced fresh ginger
- 24 white button mushrooms
- 1 large red bell pepper, cut into 12 pieces

## Peanut Sauce

- 1 can (14 ounces) unsweetened coconut milk
- ½ cup smooth peanut butter
- 2 tablespoons packed brown sugar
- 1 tablespoon rice vinegar
- 1 to 2 teaspoons red Thai curry paste

1. Cut tofu into 24 cubes.

2. Combine water, soy sauce, sesame oil, garlic and ginger in large resealable food storage bag. Add tofu, mushrooms and bell pepper. Turn bag gently to coat. Marinate 30 minutes, turning occasionally. Soak eight 8-inch bamboo skewers in water 20 minutes.

3. Preheat oven to 400°F. Drain tofu mixture; discard marinade. Thread vegetables and tofu onto skewers.

4. Spray 13×9-inch baking pan with nonstick cooking spray. Place skewers in baking pan. Bake 25 minutes or until tofu cubes are lightly browned and vegetables are softened.

5. Meanwhile, whisk coconut milk, peanut butter, brown sugar, vinegar and curry paste in small saucepan over medium heat. Bring to a boil, stirring constantly. Immediately reduce heat to low; cook about 20 minutes over very low heat, stirring often, until creamy and thick. Serve satay with sauce.

*Makes 4 servings*

## nutrients per serving:

| | |
|---|---|
| **Calories** 625 | **Total Fat** 49g |
| **Calories from Fat** 67% | **Saturated Fat** 26g |
| **Protein** 24g | **Cholesterol** 0mg |
| **Carbohydrate** 29g | **Sodium** 1,609mg |
| **Fiber** 7g | |

# Spinach

Spinach makes it easy to go green. It's delicious raw or cooked, available year round and packed with nutrients, including iron and vitamin E.

## benefits

Maybe spinach won't give you biceps like Popeye, but it is one of the world's healthiest vegetables. It provides generous helpings of vitamins A, C and E, plus more than a dozen phytonutrients that help fight inflammation, heart disease and cancer. Of special interest to those on a plant-based diet is the fact that spinach is rich in calcium and iron. The sort of iron in spinach is difficult for the body to absorb, but this can be improved by enjoying it with vitamin C rich foods—oranges, grapefruit, strawberries or tomatoes.

## selection and storage

There are three main varieties of spinach. The most common has flat rounded leaves and is called smooth or flat spinach. Savoy spinach is more likely to be available at farmers' markets and has crinkly, curly leaves that are somewhat spear shaped. Semi-savoy varieties are halfway in between and are generally the easiest, most disease resistant plants to grow at home. Spinach does not do well in warm weather, so prime seasons are early spring and fall. All varieties should have crisp, dark green leaves. Some may have reddish veins. Avoid bunches of spinach with yellowing wilted leaves or those riddled with tears and holes. Dirt on the leaves is NOT a bad sign. Frozen spinach is readily available.

## preparation

The most difficult step in cooking spinach is washing it. Because it grows so close to the ground it is often splashed with mud, grit and sand. The best method is to fill a large bowl or salad spinner with water. Discard any tough stems. Swish the leaves around and lift them out. Repeat the process until no dirt is left behind in the bowl. To keep spinach from flying all over your cutting board, stack the leaves and roll them into a cylinder before slicing.

## recipe suggestions

Salads, stir-fries and pasta dishes can all get a nutritional boost with the addition of spinach. Because spinach only needs minutes to wilt, it can be added at the last minute to grain or rice dishes. It also makes a nice change from lettuce on sandwiches.

# penne pasta with chunky tomato sauce and spinach

- 8 ounces multigrain penne pasta
- 2 cups spicy marinara sauce
- 1 large ripe tomato, chopped (about 1½ cups)
- 4 cups packed baby spinach or torn spinach leaves (4 ounces)
- ¼ cup grated dairy-free Parmesan cheese alternative
- ¼ cup chopped fresh basil

1. Cook pasta according to package directions. Drain and keep warm.

2. Meanwhile, heat marinara sauce and tomato in medium saucepan over medium heat 3 to 4 minutes or until hot and bubbly, stirring occasionally. Remove from heat; stir in spinach.

3. Add sauce to pasta; toss to combine. Top with dairy-free cheese and basil.

*Makes 4 servings*

## nutrients per serving:

**Calories** 296
**Calories from Fat** 9%
**Protein** 14g
**Carbohydrate** 56g
**Fiber** 10g
**Total Fat** 4g
**Saturated Fat** 0g
**Cholesterol** 0mg
**Sodium** 582mg

# Sweet Potatoes

Let's give thanks for sweet potatoes! With their rich flavor and smooth texture, they deserve to be on our tables year round, not just at Thanksgiving.

## benefits

First of all, you should know that sweet potatoes are NOT potatoes or yams. In fact they are not related to regular potatoes or to true yams, which are an entirely different species and very rarely sweet. No matter—whatever you call them, the lovely orange color in a sweet potato is a sign of their high content of beta-carotene, an antioxidant that converts to vitamin A in your body. They're also high in fiber and vitamin C, and best of all, they keep your sweet tooth satisfied without a lot of calories.

## selection and storage

There are more than 100 varieties of sweet potatoes. Skin colors range from white to red to copper to purplish-pink. Their flesh comes in shades of orange, yellow, purple and red.

Most sweet potatoes grown here are Beauregard, Jewell or Garnet varieties—all orange-fleshed and fairly sweet. If you see smaller, oddly shaped sweet potatoes at the farmers' market, snap them up. They are incredibly flavorful, skin and all. All sweet potatoes should be firm and free of decay. They are more perishable than they look, and once bruised rapidly deteriorate. Store them in a dry, dark, cool place, not the refrigerator. Use them within a week. Cooked sweets can be stored in the refrigerator in a covered container for up to five days.

## preparation

Scrub sweet potatoes before cooking and leave the skin on to prevent loss of nutrients and lock in natural sweetness. Pierce the skin with a fork before baking to allow steam to escape. Be careful when slicing a large specimen before cooking. Steady it on a large cutting board and use a sharp knife.

## recipe suggestions

Whole sweet potatoes can be baked at 400°F for 40 to 50 minutes. To speed things up, start by microwaving for 3 or 4 minutes. Sauté sliced or diced sweet potatoes in olive oil for about 10 minutes. For fries, peel and cut into sticks, then bake until tender. Thick slices can be brushed with oil and grilled.

# spicy african chickpea and sweet potato stew

        Spice Paste (recipe follows)
1½ pounds sweet potatoes, peeled and
        cubed
2 cups vegetable broth or water
1 can (about 15 ounces) chickpeas, rinsed
        and drained
1 can (about 14 ounces) plum tomatoes,
        undrained, chopped
1½ cups sliced fresh okra *or* 1 package
        (10 ounces) frozen cut okra, thawed
        Prepared couscous
        Hot pepper sauce

1. Prepare Spice Paste.

2. Combine sweet potatoes, broth, chickpeas, tomatoes with juice, okra and Spice Paste in large saucepan. Bring to a boil over high heat. Reduce heat to low. Cover and simmer 15 minutes. Uncover; simmer 10 minutes or until vegetables are tender.

3. Serve stew over couscous with hot pepper sauce.                    *Makes 4 servings*

## spice paste

        6 cloves garlic, peeled
        1 teaspoon coarse salt
        2 teaspoons paprika
1½ teaspoons whole cumin seeds
        1 teaspoon black pepper
        ½ teaspoon ground ginger
        ½ teaspoon ground allspice
        1 tablespoon olive oil

Process garlic and salt in blender or small food processor until garlic is finely chopped. Add remaining seasonings. Process 15 seconds. With blender running, pour in oil through cover opening; process until mixture forms paste.

## nutrients per serving:

**Calories** 546
**Calories from Fat** 11%
**Protein** 16g
**Carbohydrate** 107g
**Fiber** 14g
**Total Fat** 7g
**Saturated Fat** 1g

**Cholesterol** 0mg
**Sodium** 1,667mg

# Swiss Chard

With its beautiful ruffled leaves and gaudy multi-colored stems, Swiss chard is one of the loveliest vegetables. That pretty exterior hides a slightly sweet, earthy flavor and powerful nutrition.

## benefits

Swiss chard (or just chard) is related to beets and spinach, so it's not surprising that it is a nutritional powerhouse. Chard leaves contain 13 beneficial phytonutrients, which may help prevent spikes in blood sugar after a meal. It is also an excellent source of vitamins K, A and C, as well as fiber. As if that weren't enough, chard has a good amount of protein, calcium and magnesium. How do all those nutrients fit in those dainty leaves? Chard is like getting two vegetables in one, so don't discard those crisp, juicy stems. They can be cooked with the leaves or cooked on their own in similar ways to asparagus.

## selection and storage

The best chard is fresh chard—high season is June through October. There are several varieties of chard. Leaves are always green, but sometimes very wrinkled, sometimes smoother. Stems and veins can be red, yellow or white. Rainbow chard offers a variety of different colored stems in each bunch. White stemmed chard has thicker, flatter stems, which are ideal if you prefer the crisp parts or want a bigger yield. (The leaves shrink like spinach; the stems hold their shape.) For the freshest chard and best selection, shop a farmers' market. The leaves should be crisp, never yellowed or soggy. Store chard, unwashed and well wrapped, in the vegetable crisper. Keep it away from apples, pears and tropical fruits, which will cause it to spoil more quickly. It should last up to five days.

## preparation

Separate chard stems from leaves, since the stems take longer to cook. Like all leafy greens, chard can hide dirt and sand in its leaves, so wash well in several changes of water.

## recipe suggestions

Swiss chard can be substituted for spinach or other greens in most recipes. Its sturdy leaves also work well as wrappers to fill with grain mixtures. Stems can be given a head start and cooked with leaves or used separately in sautéed vegetable mixtures or casseroles.

# barley and swiss chard skillet casserole

- 1 cup water
- 1 cup chopped red bell pepper
- 1 cup chopped green bell pepper
- ¾ cup uncooked quick-cooking barley
- ⅛ teaspoon garlic powder
- ⅛ teaspoon red pepper flakes
- 2 cups packed coarsely chopped Swiss chard
- 1 cup canned reduced-sodium navy beans, rinsed and drained
- 1 cup quartered cherry tomatoes
- ¼ cup chopped fresh basil leaves
- 1 tablespoon olive oil
- 2 tablespoons Italian-seasoned dry bread crumbs

1. Preheat broiler.

2. Bring water to a boil in large ovenproof skillet; add bell peppers, barley, garlic powder and red pepper flakes. Reduce heat; cover and simmer 10 minutes or until liquid is absorbed. Remove from heat.

3. Stir in chard, beans, tomatoes, basil and oil. Sprinkle with bread crumbs. Broil 2 minutes or until golden. *Makes 4 servings*

## nutrients per serving:

**Calories** 288
**Calories from Fat** 18%
**Protein** 10g
**Carbohydrate** 45g
**Fiber** 12g
**Total Fat** 6g
**Saturated Fat** <1g

**Cholesterol** 0mg
**Sodium** 488mg

# Tea

Tea has a rich and colorful history, and is very important to many cultures around the world. In fact, it is the second most consumed beverage in the world after water.

## benefits

Tea has been widely studied for years and, depending on the study you read, has been credited with preventing cancer, diabetes, heart disease and cognitive decline, as well as promoting enhanced immune function. Flavonoids, a type of antioxidant in tea, combat free radicals that can lead to cancer and heart disease. There is no downside to drinking tea, and it can be a better choice than coffee because of its potential benefits and lower caffeine content.

## selection and storage

All teas, except herbal teas, come from the Camellia sinensis plant; differences in cultivation, climate and processing result in a wide variety of tea types. White tea is made from buds and new leaves picked in early spring and is the least processed. Green tea is made from leaves that are dried soon after harvesting. Black and oolong teas are partially dried, crushed and fermented (black tea is fermented longer). Tea is very easy to flavor, allowing for many flavored varieties including Earl Grey (flavored with bergamot, a citrus fruit), vanilla, cinnamon and other spices, and fruit flavors. Chai is a generic word for tea in some languages but in the West it specifically refers to the Indian spiced tea beverage masala chai. Chai is available loose, in bags and already brewed. Herbal teas are a blend of dried herbs, flowers and spices like chamomile, mint and rooibos, an African red tea. Tea is widely available loose and in bags. Store tea separately in tightly sealed containers in a cool, dry place; it can pick up flavors from other teas, coffees or foods stored nearby.

## preparation

Brew green and white teas at a lower temperature (140° to 180°F) than black and oolong teas (195° to 212°F). Use about 1 teaspoon loose tea per 6- to 8-ounce cup, or one tea bag. Steep green teas for 1 to 3 minutes and black teas for 3 to 5 minutes.

## recipe suggestions

Serve tea hot or iced, plain or with sugar, agave, lemon or dairy-free milk. For Thai iced tea, brew a cup of jasmine tea, add a teaspoon of sugar or agave, and serve over ice with a half cup of coconut milk.

# green tea lychee frappés

1 can (15 ounces) lychees in syrup,*
   undrained
2 cups water
2 slices peeled fresh ginger (2×¼ inch)
3 green tea bags
   Fresh orange slices and cherries
   (optional)

*Canned lychees are available in the canned fruit or ethnic foods section of most supermarkets or in Asian markets.*

1. Drain lychees, reserving syrup. Place lychees in single layer in medium resealable food storage bag; freeze 1 hour or until firm. Cover syrup; refrigerate.

2. Bring water and ginger to a boil in small saucepan over medium-high heat. Cool slightly. Pour over tea bags in teapot or 2-cup heatproof measuring cup; steep 3 minutes. Discard ginger and tea bags. Cover tea; refrigerate until cool.

3. Place frozen lychees, chilled green tea and ½ cup reserved syrup in blender. Process about 20 seconds or until smooth. Pour into 2 glasses. Garnish with orange slices and cherries. Serve immediately.

*Makes 2 (10-ounce) servings*

## nutrients per serving:

**Calories** 23
**Calories from Fat** 0%
**Protein** <1g
**Carbohydrate** g
**Fiber** <1g
**Total Fat** 0g
**Saturated Fat** 0g
**Cholesterol** 0mg
**Sodium** 9mg

# Tempeh

The soybean and its various products have been a part of Asian cuisine for millennia, gradually making their way around the world. A relative newcomer to the American consumer, tempeh is a delicious Indonesian pressed soybean cake.

## benefits

Although soy products have settled into the realm of the health conscious as substitutes for meat and dairy, they should be appreciated beyond this limited use for their own merits and health benefits. Originally from Indonesia and still an important part of Javanese cuisine, tempeh is a firm cake made of cooked, fermented soybeans. The fermentation process breaks down the protein, making it more accessible to the body. Tempeh is 40 percent protein, more than tofu, and contains all eight essential amino acids. Although both tofu and tempeh are made from soybeans, they could not be more different. Where tofu is soft and squishy, tempeh is firm, chewy and textured. Tempeh has a mild nutty flavor that easily absorbs the flavors both of the food it is cooked with and sauces and marinades.

## selection and storage

Tempeh is available in the refrigerated or frozen sections of natural and health food stores and some Asian markets. Some varieties come seasoned or packed in marinade, but plain is also available.

## preparation

Tempeh is ready to eat out of the package but does benefit from cooking, especially if you plan to marinate it or use it on a sandwich. Gently simmering tempeh gives it a nice soft texture and makes it even more able to absorb the flavors of marinades or seasonings. Split the tempeh cake in half crosswise and simmer in water, broth or marinade for 10 to 15 minutes. You can use it immediately, place it in marinade or grill or fry it.

## recipe suggestions

Don't be scared to experiment with tempeh— it is versatile and sturdy and will work in just about anything you can think of. It makes a great filling for both hot and cold sandwiches and is perfect for grilling. Cut tempeh into cubes or slices and add it to stews, stir-fries and casseroles, or use crumbled or grated tempeh as a stand-in for meat in tacos and chili. Try the traditional Indonesian method of battering and frying slices and serve with a peanut satay sauce (see page 153).

# teriyaki tempeh with pineapple

- 1 package (8 ounces) unseasoned soy tempeh
- 1 cup island teriyaki sauce
- 1 cup uncooked rice
- ½ cup julienned carrots
- ½ cup snow peas
- ½ cup julienned red bell pepper strips
- 4 fresh pineapple rings

1. Halve tempeh horizontally; place in large deep skillet. Cover with water; bring to a boil over high heat. Reduce heat; simmer 10 minutes. Drain water; add 1 cup teriyaki sauce to tempeh in skillet. Simmer 10 minutes, turning tempeh occasionally. Drain and reserve teriyaki sauce; add additional sauce to make ½ cup.

2. Meanwhile, cook rice according to package directions. Heat reserved teriyaki sauce in wok or large nonstick skillet over medium-high heat. Add carrots, snow peas and bell pepper; cook and stir 4 to 6 minutes or until crisp-tender. Stir in rice. Add additional teriyaki sauce, if desired.

3. Preheat grill to medium-high. Grill tempeh and pineapple rings 5 minutes per side. Cut tempeh in half; serve with rice and pineapple. *Makes 4 servings*

**Island Tempeh Sandwich:** Omit rice and vegetables. Serve tempeh and pineapple on a soft roll with arugula, additional teriyaki sauce and vegan mayonnaise.

## nutrients per serving:

**Calories** 420
**Calories from Fat** 14%
**Protein** 20g
**Carbohydrate** 68g
**Fiber** 8g
**Total Fat** 6g
**Saturated Fat** 1g
**Cholesterol** 0mg
**Sodium** 1,862mg

# Textured Soy Protein

Also called texturized vegetable protein and most often referred to as TVP, textured soy protein is inexpensive, versatile and easy to use.

## benefits

Textured soy protein is defatted soy flour and a by-product of extracting the oil from soybeans. Reconstituted textured soy protein has a similar protein content to ground meat, around 16 percent. It easily absorbs flavors from seasonings and sauces and has a chewy texture when reconstituted that can substitute for ground meat in many recipes, making it a good choice for anyone looking to replace meat in their diet with a cholesterol-free protein source. In addition to being used as a meat substitute for vegans and vegetarians, it is also used in institutional cooking and food service to extend ground meat and lower its fat and cholesterol content.

## selection and storage

Textured soy protein comes in different shapes and sizes, depending on how it was produced. Look for it in granules, flakes, chunks and nuggets. Dried textured soy protein has a long shelf life, but once rehydrated it should be stored in the refrigerator for no more than three days or frozen for longer storage.

## preparation

Textured soy protein is very easy to use—it just needs a quick soak in hot liquid. In general, use a ratio of two parts liquid to one part dried, but check the package as larger chunks may need more liquid and some smaller granules may need less. Bring water or broth and seasonings, if desired, to a boil; pour over the textured soy protein and let stand about 10 minutes or until it's softened. It is best to rehydrate before adding to other foods so as not to affect the amount of liquid in the recipe; there's no harm in adding it dried, but you'll need plenty of liquid to spare because the textured soy protein will soak it up like a sponge. Further cooking will not hurt it; it actually benefits from simmering with other ingredients because it has time to absorb flavors.

## recipe suggestions

Use larger textured soy protein chunks in a similar fashion to cubed seitan or chicken in casseroles, soups, stews or chilis. Granular TVP is a perfect substitute for ground meat; try it in tacos, chili or Bolognese sauce, and use it to make vegan burger patties or "meat" balls.

## vegan sloppy joes

- 2 cups textured soy protein (TVP) granules
- 1¾ cups boiling water
- ½ cup ketchup
- ½ cup barbecue sauce
- 2 tablespoons cider vinegar
- 1 tablespoon brown sugar
- 1 tablespoon soy sauce
- 1 teaspoon chili powder
- 1 tablespoon olive oil
- ½ cup chopped onion
- ½ cup chopped carrot
- 4 to 6 hamburger or hot dog buns

1. Combine TVP and boiling water in large bowl; let stand 10 minutes. Combine ketchup, barbecue sauce, vinegar, brown sugar, soy sauce and chili powder in medium bowl.

2. Heat oil in large saucepan over medium-high heat. Add onion and carrot; cook and stir 5 minutes. Stir in sauce mixture; bring to a boil. Stir in reconstituted TVP and ¾ cup water. Reduce heat to low; cover and cook 20 minutes. Serve sloppy joes in buns.

*Makes 4 to 6 servings*

## nutrients per serving:

| | |
|---|---|
| **Calories** 418 | **Total Fat** 5g |
| **Calories from Fat** 12% | **Saturated Fat** 1g |
| **Protein** 30g | **Cholesterol** 0mg |
| **Carbohydrate** 62g | **Sodium** 1,098mg |
| **Fiber** 10g | |

# Tofu

There's no other ingredient like it. Tofu can be enjoyed hot or cold, stir-fried, grilled, baked or transformed into a meat, dairy or egg substitute.

## benefits

Tofu is a miracle food—high in protein, containing all of the essential amino acids, low in saturated fat with no cholesterol. Four ounces of tofu provides over 18 percent of the daily requirement for protein plus 14 percent of the daily value for omega-3 fatty acids. Tofu is sometimes called the cheese of Asia because it's made in a similar way. Soymilk is cooked and a coagulant (usually a form of calcium chloride) is added. The curds are drained and pressed into tofu.

## selection and storage

Tofu comes in many forms as a visit to any Asian market will illustrate, but there are two main types. Regular or brick tofu (sometimes called Chinese tofu) is sold in the refrigerated section of the supermarket near the dairy case and comes sealed in a plastic tub filled with water. There is usually a choice of soft, medium, firm or extra firm. Silken tofu, sometimes called Japanese tofu, has a more custard-like texture and comes in soft, medium or firm and is sometimes sold unrefrigerated in aseptic boxes. Silken tofu is an excellent thickener and works well in soups and sauces. It is too delicate to use in most stir-fries where it will crumble and dissolve.

Store regular tofu in the refrigerator; silken tofu should be refrigerated once opened. After opening, both kinds should be rinsed and transferred to a container and covered with water. Change the water daily and the tofu should remain fresh for up to a week.

Tofu can be drained and frozen for longer storage. When thawed the texture will be spongier and more absorbent.

## preparation

Pressing tofu makes it denser and easier to handle. To press tofu, cut it in half horizontally and place it between layers of paper towels. Place a weighted cutting board on top and let it stand 15 to 30 minutes.

## recipe suggestions

Tofu may be the most versatile ingredient in the world. Add cubes of tofu to salads or soups. Use it instead of dairy in creamy dips, dressings and sauces. Marinate tofu "steaks" for the grill. Add tofu cubes to marinara sauce near the end of cooking or crumble it into Italian-style pasta dishes for faux ricotta.

# ma po tofu

- 1 package (about 14 ounces) firm tofu, drained and pressed
- 2 tablespoons soy sauce
- 2 teaspoons minced fresh ginger
- 1 cup vegetable broth, divided
- 2 tablespoons black bean sauce
- 1 tablespoon sweet chili sauce
- 1 tablespoon cornstarch
- 2 tablespoons vegetable oil
- 1 green bell pepper, cut into bite-size pieces
- 2 cloves garlic, minced
- 1½ cups broccoli florets
- ¼ cup chopped fresh cilantro (optional)
  Hot cooked rice

1. Cut tofu into cubes. Place in shallow dish; sprinkle with soy sauce and ginger.

2. Stir together ¼ cup broth, black bean sauce, chili sauce and cornstarch in small bowl; set aside.

3. Heat oil in wok or large skillet over high heat. Add green pepper and garlic; cook and stir 2 minutes. Add remaining ¾ cup broth and broccoli. Bring to a boil. Reduce heat; cover and simmer 3 minutes or until broccoli is crisp-tender.

4. Stir sauce mixture and add to wok. Cook and stir 1 minute or until sauce boils and thickens. Stir in tofu mixture and simmer, uncovered, until heated through. Sprinkle with cilantro. Serve with rice.

*Makes 4 servings*

# Tomatillos

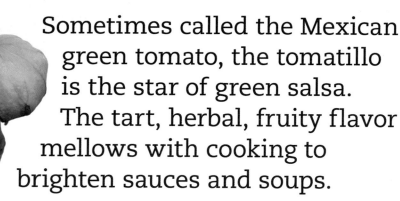

Sometimes called the Mexican green tomato, the tomatillo is the star of green salsa. The tart, herbal, fruity flavor mellows with cooking to brighten sauces and soups.

## benefits

Like its distant tomato cousin, tomatillos (pronounced "tohm-ah-TEE-ohs") are fruits used as a vegetable. Unlike tomatoes, they are covered with a papery husk. Tomatillos are low in calories and contain a good amount of vitamin C, fiber and minerals, including potassium and iron.

## selection and storage

Fresh tomatillos are easiest to find in markets that cater to a Latin American population. Look for small tomatillos, about the size of a plum, with the papery light brown husk tightly covering the fruit. They should be dry and firm without brown spots. Tomatillos do eventually ripen to yellow, but are usually sold when they are green and firm. There is also a purple variety, which has a good flavor but becomes brown when cooked. Refrigerate tomatillos in a paper bag for up to three weeks. Canned tomatillos are also available in some large supermarkets. They can be substituted for fresh, although the flavor will be different. Canned tomatillos are already husked and cooked, so if you are substituting skip those steps.

## preparation

The first step in using fresh tomatillos is removing the husk. It peels off easily. Rinse the tomatillos to remove the stickiness on their surface. Tomatillos are used both raw and cooked, like tomatoes. Many recipes call for roasting them to concentrate their flavor. Roast tomatillos under a preheated broiler for about 8 minutes until they are softened and charred in spots. You can also char them in a dry heavy skillet on the stovetop over medium heat. Blanching will mellow their flavor. Cook husked tomatillos in boiling salted water for 5 minutes or until softened.

## recipe suggestions

Make a guacamole with tomatillos replacing some of the avocados to add a fresh flavor and reduce calories. Cooked and puréed tomatillos can be blended with herbs and used as an all-purpose sauce or dip. Use them with tomatoes in juices, soups or a Bloody Mary.

## tomatillo salsa

- 1 **pound fresh tomatillos (about 12 large)** *or*
  1 **can (13 ounces) tomatillos**
- ½ **cup finely chopped red onion**
- ¼ **cup coarsely chopped fresh cilantro**
- 2 **jalapeño peppers or serrano chiles,**
  **seeded and minced**
- 1 **tablespoon lime juice**
- 1 **teaspoon olive oil**
- ½ **teaspoon salt**

1. If using fresh tomatillos, remove papery husks; wash and finely chop. If using canned tomatillos, drain; coarsely chop.

2. Combine all ingredients in medium bowl. Cover and refrigerate at least 1 hour for flavors to blend.          *Makes about 1½ cups*

**Note:** Fresh tomatillos give you a crunchy salsa; canned tomatillos make a juicier relish.

# Tomatoes

No other vegetable (or is it a fruit?) is so well loved. Tomatoes lend their bright color and balanced sweetness to many favorites—salads, pasta, chili, salsa and more.

## benefits

The tomato is botanically a fruit, but it is usually considered a vegetable in cooking since it is used in savory dishes. Tomatoes are off the chart when it comes to beneficial antioxidants. Lycopene is the most studied and seems to reduce the risk of cardiovascular disease and prostate cancer. Tomatoes are also a very good source of vitamins A, C and K, as well as potassium. This is one sweet super food that's easy to enjoy every day!

## selection and storage

There are over 7,000 tomato varieties with colors ranging from green stripes to dark purples.

They can be smaller than a grape or weigh several pounds. The best way to judge whether a tomato is ripe is to use your nose. No aroma usually means no flavor. Don't expect much from supermarket tomatoes, especially in the dead of winter. Heirloom tomatoes, which are much more fragile and can't be shipped or held for long, are much more flavorful. All tomatoes should be heavy for their size with taut skin. Heirloom varieties look a lot less perfect than supermarket specimens, so don't be put off by a spot or crack. Never store tomatoes in the refrigerator. It kills flavor and turns the flesh mealy. Canned tomatoes are an excellent option in the winter, but check labels. Some contain a lot of sodium and/or preservatives. Once opened, canned tomatoes should be transferred to a non-metal container and refrigerated for up to four days.

## preparation

To peel fresh tomatoes, first cut out the stem. Using tongs or a slotted spoon, dip the tomato into boiling water for about 15 seconds. Remove the tomato to ice water to cool. The skin should slip off easily. To remove seeds, cut the tomato in half, squeeze gently over a bowl and nudge out the seeds with your finger.

## recipe suggestions

Try different colors and varieties of tomatoes to add interest to ordinary dishes. Roast tomatoes to concentrate flavor and sweetness. Hollow out cherry tomatoes and fill with hummus for an appetizer. Serve a salad of sliced fresh tomatoes and avocados for an easy and attractive first course.

## nutrients per serving:

**Calories** 703
**Calories from Fat** 38%
**Protein** 16g

**Carbohydrate** 93g
**Fiber** 6g
**Total Fat** 30g

**Saturated Fat** 4g
**Cholesterol** 0mg
**Sodium** 120mg

## summer spaghetti

    1 pound fresh plum tomatoes, coarsely
        chopped
    1 medium onion, chopped
    6 pitted green olives, chopped
    2 cloves garlic, minced
  ⅓ cup chopped fresh parsley
    2 tablespoons finely shredded fresh basil
    2 teaspoons drained capers
  ½ teaspoon paprika
  ¼ teaspoon dried oregano leaves
    1 tablespoon red wine vinegar
  ½ cup olive oil
    1 pound uncooked spaghetti

**1.** Combine tomatoes, onion, olives, garlic, parsley, basil, capers, paprika and oregano in medium bowl; toss well. Drizzle with oil and vinegar; mix well. Let stand at room temperature 1 hour.

**2.** Just before serving, cook spaghetti according to package directions; drain well. Immediately toss hot pasta with marinated tomato sauce.  *Makes 4 to 6 servings*

# Tortillas

Tortillas originated in the time of the Aztecs when the recipe was simply corn plus water. Now tortillas come in dozens of flavors, sizes and forms.

## benefits

Tortillas are America's favorite flatbread—versatile, affordable and delicious, whether in a crisp taco or wrapped around a grilled veggie sandwich. Corn tortillas are made of corn treated with lime (calcium hydroxide, not the fruit). This unique process produces niacin, which is missing in untreated corn. Flour tortillas, more common here than in Mexico, are thinner and easier to wrap. Which is healthier? Flour tortillas are usually larger, higher in calories and fat, and often contain additives, but have more protein. Both corn and flour have their place in your kitchen, unless you are gluten sensitive, in which case, corn tortillas are your only option.

## selection and storage

Freshness is important in tortillas, as with any bread, and shelf-life varies greatly depending on the type of tortilla and its ingredients. If you live in an area with a large Mexican population, look for locally produced corn tortillas, which often are a real bargain as well as being fresher than national brands. Check the ingredient lists, especially when purchasing flour tortillas. They may contain saturated fat or artificial colors or flavors and are sometimes high in sodium.

## preparation

All tortillas should be heated to make them soft and pliable as well as bring out their flavor. There are several methods that work and all require keeping the tortillas moist so they don't dry out. In the microwave, stack tortillas separated by damp paper towels and microwave for about 30 seconds. In an oven preheated to 250°F, place a stack of tortillas wrapped in a damp kitchen towel in a covered dish. Warm for 20 minutes. Tortillas can also be heated on a griddle. Once heated, keep them hot by transferring them to a tortilla warmer or a warmed plate covered with a warm, damp kitchen towel.

## recipe suggestions

Burritos, tacos and enchiladas are just the beginning. Stack tortillas in a casserole with a mushroom-tomato or other filling in between and bake until bubbly. Or brush with oil, sprinkle with spices and bake in a hot oven for homemade tortilla chips. Tortilla chips add crunch to salads and don't forget tortilla soup!

## nutrients per serving:

**Calories** 192
**Calories from Fat** 19%
**Protein** 19g

**Carbohydrate** 20g
**Fiber** 3g
**Total Fat** 4g

**Saturated Fat** <1g
**Cholesterol** 0mg
**Sodium** 814mg

## seitan fajitas

- 1 packet (1 ounce) fajita seasoning
- 2 packages (8 ounces each) seitan,* sliced
- 1 tablespoon vegetable oil
- 1 red bell pepper, sliced
- ½ medium onion, sliced
- 1 package (8 ounces) sliced mushrooms
- 6 (6- to 7-inch) tortillas, warmed
    Salsa or guacamole or shredded
       dairy-free cheese alternative (optional)

*See page 142 for more information.*

1. Dissolve seasoning according to package directions. Place seitan in large resealable food storage bag. Pour seasoning mixture over seitan. Seal bag; shake to coat.

2. Heat oil in large skillet. Add pepper and onion; cook and stir 4 to 5 minutes or until crisp-tender. Add mushrooms; cook and stir 1 to 2 minutes or until mushrooms are softened. Add seitan and seasoning mixture; cook and stir 1 to 2 minutes or until seitan is heated through and vegetables are coated with seasoning.

3. Divide vegetable mixture evenly among tortillas. Serve with desired condiments.

*Makes 6 fajitas*

# Turmeric

Turmeric lends its golden hue to curry powder, mustard and some cheeses. This relative of ginger has a warm, slightly bitter flavor and a long history as a healing remedy.

## benefits

Like ginger, turmeric is a rhizome that is often dried and ground into a powder. It has a long history of being used as a medicine in Chinese and Indian practices and is used to treat a wide variety of conditions, including jaundice, indigestion, inflammation, chest pain and colic. Recent studies seem to affirm the anti-inflammatory effects of turmeric and more are under way, including new studies investigating turmeric's potential as a treatment for Alzheimer's disease. Turmeric is sometimes called Indian saffron because of its deep yellow-orange color, which is similar to the much more expensive spice. (The flavor is quite different, however.)

## selection and storage

Fresh turmeric can sometimes be found in Indian and Southeast Asian markets. The tiny cylindrical rhizomes have an orange-tinged beige-brown skin and can be straight or curved and knobby. Fresh turmeric has a milder, more complex flavor than the dried spice. Turmeric powder is much more readily available. Purchase from an ethic store or spice market with a high turnover to get the best price and the freshest product. Check to see that you are buying 100 percent turmeric. While turmeric is an ingredient in many curry powders, they won't contain as much of the beneficial curcumin pigment. Light and heat are enemies of dried turmeric. Keep it in a tightly sealed tin and write a date on the container so you can remember when it was purchased. It will only keep it's potency for about six months.

## preparation

Turmeric is used as a dye for a very good reason—it stains whatever it touches! Don't touch your clothing or allow it to penetrate porous countertops or cutting boards. When experimenting with adding turmeric to recipes, remember that it actually becomes stronger when cooked.

## recipe suggestions

Turmeric is a necessary ingredient in many Indian and Middle Eastern recipes and goes particularly well with rice and lentils. Add additional turmeric to recipes calling for curry powder to get more of its health benefits. Use turmeric where you wish to add a sunny, golden color to tofu or grain dishes.

## vegetarian paella

- 2 teaspoons canola oil
- 1 cup chopped onion
- 2 cloves garlic, minced
- 2¼ cups vegetable broth
- 1 can (14½ ounces) no-salt-added stewed tomatoes
- 1 cup uncooked brown rice
- 1 cup chopped red bell pepper
- 1 small zucchini, sliced
- 2 teaspoon Italian seasoning
- 1 teaspoon ground turmeric
- ⅛ teaspoon ground red pepper
- 1 can (14 ounces) quartered artichoke hearts, drained
- ½ cup frozen baby peas
- ¾ teaspoon salt (optional)

**Slow Cooker Directions**

**1.** Heat oil in medium nonstick skillet over medium-high heat. Add onion; cook and stir 6 to 7 minutes or until tender. Stir in garlic; transfer to slow cooker.

**2.** Stir broth, tomatoes, rice, bell pepper, zucchini, Italian seasoning, turmeric and ground red pepper into slow cooker. Cover; cook on LOW 4 hours or on HIGH 2 hours or until liquid is absorbed.

**3.** Stir in artichokes and peas. Season with salt, if desired. Cover; cook 5 to 10 minutes or until vegetables are tender.

*Makes 6 servings*

# Vegetable Broth

Vegetable broth is an essential vegan pantry staple. It adds flavor to all kinds of foods and magically makes many recipes vegan. Simply substitute vegetable broth for meat broth and voila, vegan!

## benefits

It can be tricky for vegans to get hearty and delicious soups and stews. Vegans have to be careful when eating out because even if a soup or stew sounds vegan, it is probably made with meat broth (just ask French onion soup). Also, many canned soups that appear to be vegan are actually made with chicken broth or contain Parmesan cheese, so always check labels. Fortunately, vegan soups and stews are easy to prepare at home. In addition to the variety of vegan recipes available, many recipes are easy to convert to vegan by simply eliminating the meat or dairy and substituting vegetable broth for chicken or beef broth.

## selection and storage

Prepared vegetable broth is the most convenient option and also the easiest to find. It is available in cans and aseptic packages in the soup aisle and the organic or natural foods section of the supermarket. Vegetable bouillon cubes and powdered broth mix are also available, although they are a little harder to find. If you can't find them at the supermarket, look for these products at natural and health food stores.

## preparation

Vegetable broth is a natural base for soups, stews and chilis, but it is also useful in cooking to add extra flavor to foods that would normally be made with water. Use it to cook quinoa, risotto, rice, barley, lentils and pasta. Generally vegetable broth is very low in calories and fat free, although it does tend to be quite salty so make sure you compensate by reducing the added salt in your recipe.

## recipe suggestions

Making homemade vegetable broth is a great way to use up vegetables that are past their prime. Heat 1 tablespoon oil in a stockpot. Add onion wedges and garlic cloves with their skin, coarsely chopped carrots and celery and sauté 5 minutes. Add 8 to 12 cups of water, tomato paste or juice, if desired, fresh herb sprigs, dried herbs, whole peppercorns and salt. Bring to a boil; cover and simmer 30 minutes to one hour. Strain solids and use immediately or store in tightly sealed jars in the refrigerator for up to a week.

# slow cooker veggie stew

- 1 tablespoon vegetable oil
- ⅔ cup carrot slices
- ½ cup diced onion
- 2 cloves garlic, chopped
- 2 cans (about 14 ounces each) vegetable broth or homemade broth
- 1½ cups chopped green cabbage
- ½ cup cut green beans
- ½ cup diced zucchini
- 1 tablespoon tomato paste
- ½ teaspoon dried basil
- ½ teaspoon dried oregano leaves
- ¼ teaspoon salt

**Slow Cooker Directions**

1. Heat oil in medium skillet over medium-high heat. Add carrot, onion and garlic; cook and stir until tender.

2. Place carrot mixture and remaining ingredients in slow cooker; stir to combine. Cover; cook on LOW 8 to 10 hours or on HIGH 4 to 5 hours. *Makes 4 to 6 servings*

## nutrients per serving:

**Calories** 83
**Calories from Fat** 38%
**Protein** 3g
**Carbohydrate** 10g
**Fiber** 2g
**Total Fat** 4g
**Saturated Fat** <1g
**Cholesterol** 0mg
**Sodium** 654mg

# Walnuts

Walnuts have been cultivated and appreciated for over 7,000 years. They have a delectable flavor, a delicious crunch and provide amazing health benefits. That's it in a nutshell!

## benefits

Walnuts are unique among nuts for being predominantly composed of polyunsaturated fatty acids (PUFAs), and are a good source of those hard-to-get omega-3 fatty acids. They beat other common nuts when it comes to having beneficial antioxidants, too. And because they are high in protein and fiber, walnuts make a satisfying snack.

## selection and storage

English walnuts (sometimes called Persian walnuts) are the common variety. Black walnuts are native to the U.S., but seen infrequently since they are extremely hard to crack and have a stronger, earthier flavor. Choose whole walnuts with shells that are free from cracks and stains and feel heavy for their size. Shelled walnuts are sold packaged or in bulk bins. They should not be rubbery or shriveled. Walnuts have a high oil content so they spoil easily. Store shelled walnuts in an airtight container in the refrigerator for up to six months or the freezer for up to a year. Be careful when storing walnuts near other foods, as they easily pick up odors. If they taste bitter or off, they have probably become rancid and should be discarded.

## preparation

Once shelled, fresh walnuts are covered in a thin, flaky whitish skin. It's best to leave this intact since many nutrients are found there. To toast walnuts, spread them in a single layer on a baking sheet and bake in a preheated 350°F oven for 8 to 10 minutes or until fragrant, stirring once.

## recipe suggestions

Sprinkle chopped walnuts on your morning cereal or add them to pancake and waffle batter. Make the Middle Eastern dip/spread called mahamorrah. Combine 1 cup of walnuts, 2 cloves of garlic and a drained 8-ounce jar of roasted red peppers in a food processor. Whir to combine and then finish with a few tablespoons of pomegranate molasses or juice and enough olive oil to smooth it out. Walnuts add a nice crunch to fruit salads or try the classic addition of toasted walnuts and sliced pears to perk up a plain green salad.

# banana-walnut cookies

1½ cups all-purpose flour
1 teaspoon baking powder
1 teaspoon ground cinnamon
½ teaspoon baking soda
½ teaspoon salt
½ cup (1 stick) dairy-free margarine, softened
1 cup packed light brown sugar
  Prepared egg replacer equal to 1 egg
1 teaspoon vanilla
2 ripe mashed bananas (about ½ cup)
2 cups walnut pieces, toasted

1. Preheat oven to 350°F. Line cookie sheets with parchment paper. Sift together flour, baking powder, cinnamon, baking soda and salt in medium bowl.

2. Beat margarine and brown sugar in large bowl with electric mixer at medium speed 5 minutes or until light and fluffy. Beat in egg replacer and vanilla.

3. Add bananas; mix well. Beat in flour mixture at low speed. Stir in walnuts. Drop heaping tablespoons of dough 2 inches apart onto prepared cookie sheets.

4. Bake 12 to 13 minutes or until golden brown. Cool on cookie sheet 5 minutes. Remove to wire racks; cool completely.

*Makes 20 to 22 cookies*

## nutrients per serving:

**Calories** 202
**Calories from Fat** 49%
**Protein** 4g
**Carbohydrate** 23g
**Fiber** 1g
**Total Fat** 11g
**Saturated Fat** 2g
**Cholesterol** 0mg
**Sodium** 166mg

# Wheat Bran & Germ

The bran and the germ are nutritious parts of the wheat kernel that are removed to make white flour. Add them to your pantry and it's easy to make healthy additions to your cooking.

## benefits

Wheat bran is the outer coating of the wheat kernel; wheat germ is the central core of the grain. Each offers a different but powerful set of nutrients. The bran provides more than six grams of fiber in only one quarter of a cup. (An equal amount of bran cereal, which includes other ingredients, contains about four grams.) Bran is also a good source of B vitamins, magnesium and iron.

Wheat germ, a health food basic for decades, is rich in vitamin E and omega-3 fatty acids. It is also nearly 30 percent protein, which is comparable to, if not higher than, many meat products.

## selection and storage

Whole wheat contains both the bran and the germ, but the starchy endosperm makes up most of the kernel. Wheat bran is most often eaten in the form of bran cereals. As with any processed foods, check ingredient lists to see if there are preservatives or sugars you wish to avoid. Wheat bran is also available in unprocessed form at health food stores and online. It looks a little like beige sawdust. Wheat germ can be purchased raw or toasted and is usually sold in glass jars in the cereal aisle. Both wheat bran and germ are quite perishable. Check expiration dates and store them in a tightly sealed container in the refrigerator or freezer. If wheat bran or germ smells musty or tastes bitter, discard it.

## preparation

Since both wheat germ and bran are high-fiber foods, it's wise to start by adding small amounts to your diet and increasing this gradually. To toast raw wheat germ or bran spread it on a cookie sheet and bake at 350°F for 5 minutes. For a finer texture, grind wheat bran in your food processor.

## recipe suggestions

Wheat bran or germ can be sprinkled on hot or cold cereal or added to smoothies. Add a few tablespoons to pancake or waffle batters. Replace some of the flour in baking recipes with wheat bran or germ to improve nutrition.

# banana bran bread

1 cup bran cereal
½ cup boiling water
1⅓ cups all-purpose flour
½ cup sugar
1 teaspoon baking powder
½ teaspoon baking soda
¼ to ¾ teaspoon salt
½ teaspoon ground cinnamon
2 tablespoons vegetable oil
  Prepared egg replacer equal to 2 eggs
1 cup ripe mashed bananas
¼ cup crumbled unsweetened banana
  chips

**1.** Preheat oven to 350°F. Spray 8×4-inch loaf pan with nonstick cooking spray.

**2.** Place cereal in medium bowl; stir in boiling water and let stand 10 minutes. Combine flour, sugar, baking powder, baking soda, salt and cinnamon in large bowl. Whisk oil and egg replacer in small bowl; add to flour mixture. Stir in bran mixture and mashed bananas. Spoon batter into prepared pan. Sprinkle with banana chips.

**3.** Bake 45 to 50 minutes or until toothpick inserted into center comes out clean. Cool in pan 5 minutes. Turn out onto wire rack. Cool completely. *Makes 9 slices*

## nutrients per serving:

**Calories** 181
**Calories from Fat** 20%
**Protein** 4g
**Carbohydrate** 35g
**Fiber** 3g
**Total Fat** 4g
**Saturated Fat** <1g
**Cholesterol** 0mg
**Sodium** 212mg

# White Beans

You don't have to know beans to appreciate the creamy texture and nutty flavor of white beans. Bake them in a casserole, add them to a salad or soup, or enjoy a healthy helping of beans and greens.

## benefits

White beans are fiber superstars. A single cup of navy beans provides more than 75 percent of the recommended daily value of fiber. White beans are a good source of protein, too. In fact, combined with a whole grain, they provide protein comparable to what you'd get from meat or dairy, but without the saturated fat. Versatility is part of the picture, too. White beans are tasty hot or cold, paired with a spicy tomato sauce or simple oil and vinegar dressing.

## selection and storage

There are three main varieties of white beans—cannellini, Great Northern and navy beans—all are available canned and as dried beans. Cannellini beans are white kidney beans and a good choice when you want a bean with a creamy interior that holds it shape in a salad or ragu. Great Northern beans are slightly smaller and are shaped like baby limas. Navy beans are the smallest and are the variety most often used in baked beans. They are also a good choice for dips, soups or stews. Purchase dried beans from a market with a high turnover and store them in a cool, dry place. Use them within a year. Old beans will never soften and cook properly. Canned beans are also a convenient and nutritious option.

## preparation

See the preparation tips for kidney beans on page 93 for instructions on cooking dried beans. Beware of soaking dried beans too long at warm room temperatures since they can begin to ferment. On hot days, soak them in the refrigerator. Cannellini beans will take the longest to cook, usually a little over an hour. Great Northerns and navy beans take about an hour.

## recipe suggestions

Make a quick bean dip with olive oil and herbs to serve with chips, veggies or to use as a spread. White beans pair well with sturdy, bitter greens like broccoli rabe or mustard greens. Think Italian and make pasta e fagioli—a soup with cannellini beans and pasta.

# italian escarole and white bean stew

- 1 tablespoon olive oil
- 1 onion, chopped
- 3 carrots, cut into ½-inch slices
- 2 cloves garlic, minced
- 1 can (about 14 ounces) vegetable broth
- 1 head (about 12 ounces) escarole
- ¼ teaspoon red pepper flakes
- 2 cans (about 15 ounces each) Great Northern beans, rinsed and drained
- Salt and black pepper
- Grated dairy-free Parmesan cheese alternative (optional)

**Slow Cooker Directions**

1. Heat oil in medium skillet over medium-high heat. Add onion and carrots; cook until onion is softened, stirring occasionally. Add garlic; cook and stir 1 minute. Transfer to slow cooker. Pour in broth.

2. Trim base of escarole. Cut crosswise into 1-inch-wide strips. Wash well in large bowl of cold water and shake to remove excess water. Add to slow cooker. Sprinkle with red pepper flakes. Top with beans.

3. Cover; cook on LOW 7 to 8 hours or on HIGH 3½ to 4 hours or until escarole is wilted and very tender. Season with salt and pepper and sprinkle with cheese alternative, if desired. *Makes 4 servings*

## nutrients per serving:

| | | |
|---|---|---|
| **Calories** 332 | **Carbohydrate** 57g | **Saturated Fat** 1g |
| **Calories from Fat** 12% | **Fiber** 15g | **Cholesterol** 0mg |
| **Protein** 19g | **Total Fat** 5g | **Sodium** 743mg |

# Wine

Food and wine belong together. They have a magical synergy that makes both of them taste better. Cooking with wine is an easy way to make ordinary recipes extraordinary.

## benefits

Cooking with even a very small amount of wine provides an amazing amount of flavor. The alcohol works to extract flavors, too, much as we use alcohol to extract the flavor of vanilla beans in vanilla extract. Much, but not all, of the wine you add in cooking evaporates as the sauce simmers or the vegetables steam, so there's no reason to worry about getting drunk over dinner. Red wine, in moderation, can be heart healthy. Resveratrol is one substance in red wine that seems to help prevent damage to blood vessels.

## selection and storage

A good rule of thumb for cooking with wine is not to use anything you wouldn't drink; nor do you want to waste an expensive bottle of vintage Bordeaux in a soup or stir-fry. Lighter, less complex wines are better choices since cooking will intensify flavors. The concentrated taste of a big, tannic Chianti or super oaky Chardonnay would overwhelm any dish. Strict vegans may be concerned about the way in which a wine is filtered. Some methods involve filtering through animal-based elements like gelatin or egg whites. If this is a concern, check online where listings of vegan friendly wines are easy to find. If you have favorite wines you're unsure about, inquire at the winery or wine shop.

## preparation

Cooking with wine is an excellent way to use up leftover wine. Stash the partly empty bottle in the refrigerator and use it up within five days. Avoid products labeled "cooking wine" as they often have added salt and food coloring.

## recipe suggestions

Think of wine as an acid ingredient and use it as you would lemon juice. White wine can brighten up vegetable dishes and bring out subtle nuances of flavor. Red wine can add depth and complexity to tomato or mushroom sauces. Use a wine/olive oil marinade for tofu or portobello mushrooms headed for the grill. Wine can even be used in baking—chocolate red wine cake anyone?

# cabernet pears

- 4 pears, preferably Bosc
- 1 bottle (750 mL) Carbernet Sauvignon
- ⅓ cup plus ¼ cup sugar, divided
- 1 stick cinnamon
- 7 peppercorns
- 1 bay leaf
- 2 whole cloves
- 3 sprigs fresh thyme

**1.** Peel pears and core from bottom, leaving stem on. Place in large saucepan. Pour in wine; add water as needed to cover pears. Add ⅓ cup sugar, cinnamon, peppercorns, bay leaf, cloves and thyme.

**2.** Bring to a boil; reduce heat to a simmer. Simmer gently, uncovered, 30 to 40 minutes or until pears are fork tender.

**3.** Remove pears to serving dish; strain 2 cups of poaching liquid into saucepan and add remaining ¼ cup sugar. Bring to a boil; cook 15 to 30 minutes or until reduced to a sauce; serve over pears. *Makes 4 servings*

## nutrients per serving:

**Calories** 173
**Calories from Fat** 0%
**Protein** 1g
**Carbohydrate** 40g
**Fiber** 2g

**Total Fat** <1g
**Saturated Fat** 0g
**Cholesterol** 0mg
**Sodium** 11mg

# Zucchini

Any way you slice it, zucchini is delicious. You can sauté it in rounds, shred it into a slaw, bake it into bread, grill it in thick slabs or hollow it out and stuff it.

## benefits

Zucchini might be the most undemanding vegetable in the produce department. It's always available and affordable, has a mild flavor that works in just about any dish and cooks in a matter of minutes. It provides a powerful combination of nutrients, including vitamins A, $B_6$ and C, manganese and potassium.

## selection and storage

Zucchini is actually a plural of the Italian word "zucchino", which we use in both the singular and plural sense. (Well, have you ever seen just ONE zucchini all by itself?) The smooth, dark green zucchini is the most common variety, but there are more options every year. Golden zucchini look like ordinary zucchini painted a bright sunshine yellow. Flavorful Romanesco zucchini have pale ridges running lengthwise. There are even round zucchini, sometimes playfully referred to as "eight ball" zucchini.

Whichever variety you choose, look for skin that is smooth, taut and free of pitting. They should be firm and solid with the stem attached. Even fresh zucchini may be unevenly colored or look slightly scratched. Baby zucchini are extremely cute and zucchini flowers are edible and beautiful. You will find these only in season (May through August) at farmers' markets. Enjoy zucchini as soon as possible after purchasing. They can be stored, unwashed, in the crisper drawer for a few days.

## preparation

There's no need to peel zucchini's tender skin. Scrub with a vegetable brush to remove any dirt or prickly stubble. If you are dealing with a giant of the squash world, try salting it as you might an eggplant to draw out some of the water and then squeezing and blotting dry.

## recipe suggestions

Zucchini pairs well with other Mediterranean vegetables and herbs, like tomatoes, eggplant, peppers, basil and rosemary. Thin slices of zucchini can take the place of noodles in lasagna. Slice a zucchini into thick pieces at a slant, brush with olive oil, sprinkle with salt, pepper and Italian seasoning and grill until tender and browned in spots. Or cut it into sticks, season and bake like French fries.

# spaghetti squash with black beans and zucchini

1 spaghetti squash (about 2 pounds)
2 medium zucchini, cut lengthwise into
  ¼-inch-thick slices
  Nonstick cooking spray
2 cups chopped seeded fresh tomatoes
1 can (about 15 ounces) black beans,
  rinsed and drained
2 tablespoons chopped fresh basil
2 tablespoons olive oil
2 tablespoons red wine vinegar
1 clove garlic, minced
½ teaspoon salt

1. Prepare grill for direct cooking. Pierce spaghetti squash in several places with fork. Wrap in large piece of heavy-duty foil. Grill, covered, over medium heat 45 minutes to 1 hour or until flesh gives easily when pressed, turning a quarter turn every 15 minutes. Remove and let stand in foil 10 to 15 minutes.

2. Meanwhile, spray both sides of zucchini slices with cooking spray. Grill, uncovered, over medium heat 4 minutes or until tender, turning once. Cut into bite-size pieces.

3. Remove squash from foil and cut in half; scoop out seeds. Remove spaghetti-like strands with fork; place in serving dish and keep warm. Place tomatoes, beans, zucchini and basil in medium bowl. Combine olive oil, vinegar, garlic and salt in small bowl. Add to vegetables and toss gently to combine. Serve over spaghetti squash.          *Makes 4 servings*

## nutrients per serving:

| | |
|---|---|
| **Calories** 219 | **Cholesterol** 0mg |
| **Calories from Fat** 30% | **Sodium** 613mg |
| **Protein** 12g | |
| **Carbohydrate** 34g | |
| **Fiber** 8g | |
| **Total Fat** 8g | |
| **Saturated Fat** 1g | |

# Index

# Metric Conversion Chart

### VOLUME MEASUREMENTS (dry)

1/8 teaspoon = 0.5 mL
1/4 teaspoon = 1 mL
1/2 teaspoon = 2 mL
3/4 teaspoon = 4 mL
1 teaspoon = 5 mL
1 tablespoon = 15 mL
2 tablespoons = 30 mL
1/4 cup = 60 mL
1/3 cup = 75 mL
1/2 cup = 125 mL
2/3 cup = 150 mL
3/4 cup = 175 mL
1 cup = 250 mL
2 cups = 1 pint = 500 mL
3 cups = 750 mL
4 cups = 1 quart = 1 L

### VOLUME MEASUREMENTS (fluid)

1 fluid ounce (2 tablespoons) = 30 mL
4 fluid ounces (1/2 cup) = 125 mL
8 fluid ounces (1 cup) = 250 mL
12 fluid ounces (1 1/2 cups) = 375 mL
16 fluid ounces (2 cups) = 500 mL

### WEIGHTS (mass)

1/2 ounce = 15 g
1 ounce = 30 g
3 ounces = 90 g
4 ounces = 120 g
8 ounces = 225 g
10 ounces = 285 g
12 ounces = 360 g
16 ounces = 1 pound = 450 g

### DIMENSIONS

1/16 inch = 2 mm
1/8 inch = 3 mm
1/4 inch = 6 mm
1/2 inch = 1.5 cm
3/4 inch = 2 cm
1 inch = 2.5 cm

### OVEN TEMPERATURES

250°F = 120°C
275°F = 140°C
300°F = 150°C
325°F = 160°C
350°F = 180°C
375°F = 190°C
400°F = 200°C
425°F = 220°C
450°F = 230°C

### BAKING PAN SIZES

| Utensil | Size in Inches/Quarts | Metric Volume | Size in Centimeters |
|---|---|---|---|
| Baking or Cake Pan (square or rectangular) | 8×8×2 | 2 L | 20×20×5 |
| | 9×9×2 | 2.5 L | 23×23×5 |
| | 12×8×2 | 3 L | 30×20×5 |
| | 13×9×2 | 3.5 L | 33×23×5 |
| Loaf Pan | 8×4×3 | 1.5 L | 20×10×7 |
| | 9×5×3 | 2 L | 23×13×7 |
| Round Layer Cake Pan | 8×1½ | 1.2 L | 20×4 |
| | 9×1½ | 1.5 L | 23×4 |
| Pie Plate | 8×1¼ | 750 mL | 20×3 |
| | 9×1¼ | 1 L | 23×3 |
| Baking Dish or Casserole | 1 quart | 1 L | — |
| | 1½ quart | 1.5 L | — |
| | 2 quart | 2 L | — |